Transformed

Shaped by the Hand of God

STUART CALVERT

Woman's Missionary Union
P. O. Box 830010
Birmingham, AL 35283-0010

Dewey Decimal Classification: 248.4
Subject Headings: CHRISTIAN LIFE
                   BIBLE—STUDY AND TEACHING

Unless otherwise indicated Scripture quotations are from the
Holy Bible, New International Version. Copyright © 1973, 1978,
1984 International Bible Society. Used by permission of
Zondervan Bible Publishers.
   Scripture quotations indicated by TEV are from the *Good
News Bible,* Today's English Version. Old Testament: Copyright ©
1976 American Bible Society. New Testament: Copyright
© American Bible Society, 1966, 1971, 1976. Used by permission.
   Scripture quotations indicated by KJV are from the King
James Version of the Bible.
   Scripture quotations indicated by NKJV are from The Holy
Bible, New King James Version. Copyright ©1982 Thomas
Nelson, Inc. Used by permission.

ISBN: 1-56309-232-8

W983107•1098•4M2

Transformed

Introduction

The nurse lay the tiny human bundle in the curve of my arm. The first sight of my first son brought a rush of manifold emotions. As the years passed, the kitchen window framed his life. Through the panes, I watched him progress from a bouncy kid tugging at a kite to a strapping teenager scuffling in a neighborhood touch football game.

Through the window of a hospital nursery, I watched a nurse lay the tiny human bundle in the curve of his arm. The first sight of my first son cuddling his newborn daughter brought a rush of manifold emotions. For a split second I imagined the nursery window as the kitchen window. Memories of the changes in my son flooded my thoughts and overflowed as tears. The stages in transformation continue, overlap, and begin again.

Transformation suggests a change in shape, character, and circumstances like from a child to a man. Through the changes in our son's life, one short prayer, among many, remained constant: Lord, through the miracle of birth, he is mine. Through the miracle of rebirth, he is Yours. He resembles me but You made him unique. Give us wisdom to nurture, to mold him for You. Then make us spiritually mature enough to turn him loose to You.

God the Potter

The Bible pictures God as a Potter molding the clay of pliable personalities into unique individuals equipped for service. "But you are our father, Lord. We are like clay, and you are like the potter. You created us" (Isa. 64:8 TEV).

A summary of Jeremiah 18:1–6 describes how a potter transformed clay into a useful vessel: God sent Jeremiah to the potter's house where he saw the potter molding a vessel on a wheel. Jeremiah watched the potter crush the vessel and remold it to perfection. God spoke to Jeremiah, "You are in my hands just like clay in the potter's hands" (Jer. 18:6 TEV). In the biblical analogy the potter represents God. The clay represents people. The wheel represents the circumstances of life.

Clay is the kind of earth composed of extremely fine particles. When a human potter designs a particular vessel, he carefully chooses clay separated from the impurities of mud and sand. The combination of a variety of minerals produce different textures and colors of clay suitable for different kinds of containers. For example, the potter selects the purest clay, kaolin, for fine porcelain pieces or clay free of iron for inexpensive crockery.

God, the Potter, had a thought in mind for a special kind of vessel. He looked at the available clay and chose you. You are the clay to which He wanted to transfer His thought. When a sculptor chips an image from marble, bits and pieces of rock clutter the space. When a carver whittles into being a wooden object, shavings pile up around his bench. But the potter does not reduce the substance. He bends, shapes, and transforms the whole lump of clay into a vessel. God uses all your experiences and relationships to mold a useful vessel.

Perhaps God looks at us as we look at newborns through a nursery window. Even before the parental touch soothes the stress of exiting the chrysalis womb, before the discipline shapes coping skills for entering a carnal world, we believe our child will fulfill our most magnanimous dreams. We believe in the wiggly, wrinkled infant's potential.

You had no innate power to realize your potential. God saw possibilities in your clay for a one and only kind of vessel. Your uniqueness is a foundation for developing a high self-esteem. We are not products of an assembly line. Each vessel is meticulously crafted for a particular service. In a china boutique or a pottery store, certain vessels attract our attention. Likewise in the community, different kinds of Christian vessels attract people who need a witness or who need a ministry. Your vessel may draw the attention of someone who never has met the Potter. "For we are His workmanship, created in Christ Jesus for good works, which God prepared beforehand that we should walk in them" (Eph. 2:10 NKJV).

As a human potter prepares the clay for the wheel, he sometimes must expose difficult clay to the weather. In like manner, God, the Potter, kneads human clay through discipline and training to work out character flaws. Hebrews 12:5–11 explains how we should respond to God's discipline: "And you have forgotten that word of encouragement that addresses you as sons:

"My son, do not make light of the Lord's discipline, and do not lose heart when he rebukes you, because the Lord disciplines those he loves, and he punishes everyone he accepts as a son.

"Endure hardship as discipline; God is treating you as sons. For what son is not disciplined by his father? If you are not disciplined (and everyone undergoes discipline), then you are illegitimate children and not true sons. Moreover, we have all had human fathers who disciplined us and we respected them for it. How much more should we submit to the Father of our spirits and live! Our fathers disciplined us for a little while as they thought best; but God disciplines us for our good, that we may share in his holiness. No discipline seems pleasant at the time, but painful. Later on, however, it produces a harvest of righteousness and peace for those who have been trained by it."

A knowledgeable collector of china admired the fine pieces on display. He chose to buy an exquisite cup expecting to pay an expensive price for the item. The salesperson asked only for 50 cents. Startled, the collector protested that the cup must be of more value. The salesperson explained that a flaw diminished the value. Examining the cup, the collector in disbelief said, "I don't see any flaw." The salesperson told him that the potter saw the flaw and would not sell the cup for the intended price.

Even though others may shower us with compliments, Jesus sees the flaws.[1] Rather than abandoning us, He remolds us. Samson's life shows how God's chastisement remolds fatal character flaws. God planned for Samson to be a judge in Israel. Physically macho but morally weak, Samson succumbed to Delilah's devilish wiles. He divulged the secret of his strength, "'No razor has ever been used on my head,' he said, 'because I have been a Nazirite set apart to God since birth. If my head were shaved, my strength would leave me, and I would become as weak as any other man'" (Judg. 16:17).

Delilah called for a man to shave off Samson's seven braids, depleting his strength (Judg. 16:19). His Philistine enemies gouged out his eyes with a hot iron, and threw him into prison. A broken man, Samson ground meal in the darkness. But his hair began to grow (16:21–22). One day the Philistines gathered in the temple and called on Samson for entertainment. Placed between two supporting columns, Samson stretched out his arms and prayed for strength to slay the Philistines. Samson brought down the temple, killing thousands of his enemies (16:25–30). In the waning moments of Samson's life, God remolded him and renewed the power of His servant. Any time in life is a good time to be remolded!

Soft clay bends too easily. Clay that is too wet warps. Only properly mixed clay will retain its shape. To strengthen weak clay, a human potter often adds pulverized, fired pottery to the material. Blending the old with the new firms the clay. In like manner, God mixes and blends all of life's experiences to make our personal clay productive and resilient. God kneads into our clay spiritual qualities. Second Peter 1:5–8 suggests a few of these qualities: "For this very reason, make every effort to add to your faith goodness; and to goodness, knowledge; and to knowledge, self-control;

and to self-control, perseverance; and to perseverance, godliness; and to godliness, brotherly kindness; and to brotherly kindness, love. For if you possess these qualities in increasing measure, they will keep you from being ineffective and unproductive in your knowledge of our Lord Jesus Christ."[2]

A human potter rests the clay to even the texture. The result is a pliable clay that will not crack on the wheel. God recognizes that rest for human clay is necessary for transformation. Rest evens the texture of life by replenishing our minds, emotions, souls, and bodies. Not recognizing that God is resting us, we consider inactivity a waste of time. We become anxious and annoyed. Abraham was 75 years old when God announced His purpose for Abraham's life. Sarah and Abraham waited 25 more years for Isaac's birth. They became impatient and questioned the waiting period. Thinking of ourselves as clay, we confidently rest knowing that God, the Potter, molds carefully and desires the best for us. He knows the preparation we need. Yet He waits for our response to each step in the process before continuing to the next step. Through a slow tedious process, the clay relinquishes its identity and yields to the Potter's hand.

God, the Potter, placed you on the wheel of life's circumstances. With His design for you in mind, He began the rhythm of the wheel. It turns through many experiences. The difficult ones soften the spirit to better receive divine impressions. More often, the wheel spins you through mundane circumstances. The meaning of circumstance combines two words: *circum* (around) and *stance* (to stand). Remain in the circle through repetitious routines, and you will be refined.[3]

Human clay, unlike earthy clay, can question, complain, and refuse to respond. Israel's question humbles a haughty attitude: "Does a clay pot dare argue with its maker, a pot that is like all the others? Does the clay ask the potter what he is doing? Does the pot complain that its maker has no skill?" (Isa. 45:9 TEV). Comparing your vessel to others, complaining to the Potter about the design of your vessel is an affront to His sovereignty. Paul rebukes our impudence in Romans 9:20–21: "But who are you, O man, to talk back to God? Shall what is formed say to him who formed it, 'Why did you make me like this?' Does not the potter have the right to make out of the same lump of clay some pottery for noble purposes and some for common use?" Job reminds us, "You and I are the same in God's sight, both of us were formed from clay" (Job 33:6 TEV).

Because of your place on the wheel, you do not understand the complete plan. What a comfort to know that despite crises, confusion, and changes in life, God controls the wheel. The wheel has no affect on the clay apart from the pressure of the potter's hand or foot.

God, the Potter, focuses His full attention on bringing your vessel into being. Life situations may scratch and scar human vessels. What may seem like a defect or blemish may be your strength. Appearances do not determine our ability to serve. When Samuel journeyed to Bethlehem to anoint a king, he liked the looks of Jesse's son, Eliab. Samuel thought, "Surely the Lord's anointed stands here before the Lord" (1 Sam. 16:6).

Appearances deceive and so the Lord spoke to Samuel, "Do not consider his appearance or his height, for I have rejected him. The Lord does not look at the things man looks at. Man looks at the outward appearance, but the Lord looks at the heart" (16:7). How we look does not determine our worth. God's acknowledgment, acceptance, and appreciation give worth to the clay.

The Duck Bowl
Ducks lived among a menagerie of pets I cared for as a child. When I asked my grandmother for a water bowl for the ducks, she pointed to a chipped white bowl saying, "Take the pitcher out of that old bowl and use it."

Time passed. Our antique furnishings that I had considered ugly became handsome and cherished heirlooms. At some point, I remembered the duck bowl. In the yard where I had placed it 15 years before, I kicked through the pine straw, debris, and dirt until I touched the rim of the bowl. I carefully freed it from the earth, rinsed it clean, and glued the cracks. The abuse of time, weather, and duck pecks had marred the bowl. But it is not useless.

The duck bowl never will hold water. The duck bowl holds memories. At this moment, I see the bowl and pitcher, reunited, in a prominent place on an antique commode. I remember the fun of watering the ducks, the security of playing in a pine grove, the intimate conversations between the Lord and me walking among the trees. Other vessels in my home hold water. Only the duck bowl holds past memories of life's experiences that the Lord blends into the present to make my clay more productive. Only the duck bowl holds early memories of moments when I felt God's transforming touch on my life.

One of the memories held in the duck bowl relates to the Lord's initial impression that He would mold me to communicate through writing. Although words fascinated me, I only intended to use a few in an occasional friendly letter. I never considered expressing thoughts or feelings for publication. During the first year of my volunteer involvement with the juvenile court, our Woman's Missionary Union® (WMU®) executive director asked me to write about the experience for her to use in publicizing Round Table groups in our state. A study of juvenile delinquency in a Round Table group had catapulted me into the juvenile rehabilitation ministry. Marjean, our director, sent the article to the editor of *Royal Service*, and the editor invited me to write the Round Table study session for one month. Surprised by the request, I walked through the pine grove to my favorite spot. Kneeling, I spread the letter on the straw and read it aloud. In the dirt, I drew a vertical line labeling one side pro and the other con. Talking honestly to the Lord, I listed the reasons I could and could not write. After a long struggle scrutinizing the weaknesses and strengths, His simple, distinctive direction surfaced in my mind: What I need is an empty mind and a hand to hold a pen. Such a relief! I qualified for both needs!

Like a human potter, God shapes us from within through the power of the Holy Spirit. "And we, who with unveiled faces all reflect the Lord's glory, are being transformed into his likeness with ever-increasing

glory, which comes from the Lord, who is the Spirit"
(2 Cor. 3:18). The same hand that exerts pressure
within the container to shape us also supports us. With
God, the Potter, the partially formed vessel is as much
in His will as the vessel that has served the Lord for
many years. All of us are in the process of becoming.

Stretching is an important step in forming the clay
into a vessel. By pulling up the clay and pressing it
down, the potter tames unsteady clay. God, the Potter,
stretches our human clay. We experience high moments of joy and ecstasy followed by the depths of dol-
drums. Before God raised Moses to lead the Israelites,
He lowered Moses to the shepherd in Midian.

A profitable exercise is to chart the ups and downs
of a segment of your life. The visual illustrates how
backsets are steps toward progress. As you chart the
stretches in your life, remember Romans 8:28: "And we
know that in all things God works for the good of those
who love him, who have been called according to his
purpose." Struggles strengthen the finished vessel.

Movement on the tree limb caught the attention of
the hiker. He recognized the emergence of a butterfly
from the hard shell of the cocoon. Fascinated, the hiker
watched the butterfly shiver and struggle to free itself
for a life of flight. Intending to help the butterfly, he
clipped a minute piece of the chrysalis. The butterfly
emerged with a scarred wing and a weaker body because of the shorter struggle. The metamorphosis of a
caterpillar into a butterfly requires a great effort against
difficulties.[4]

God, the Potter, is not a tyrant. He will not force us to
conform to His molding. Grit from sin or stubbornness

in the clay resists His authority. Perverting God's purpose is a possibility. For example, God had great career plans for Saul. But Saul chose his own path leading to a pathetic end. A sad fact is that repeated resistance to God's molding makes the clay less and less pliable. While your clay is still supple, yield to God. One day might be too late. Jeremiah demonstrated God's judgment by throwing a jar onto the rocks. The hardened vessel could not be remolded. Being broken into pieces made reshaping impossible (Jer. 19).

Stepping outside of the potter's house, you will find yourself in the potter's field. You will hear crunching of broken crockery under your feet. These broken pieces of clay are fragments of vessels that might have been.

God's intention is to salvage us, to refashion us into worthy vessels. Jeremiah saw the potter crush the marred vessel, replace it on the wheel, and mold it into another vessel—a new beginning, a fresh start.

God remolds us while we are in motion on the wheel of life's circumstances. Imperfect yet yielded people who are working and serving are more responsive to God's touch than those sulking on the sidelines waiting for a grand opportunity to impact society. When we defy God's plan, He does not give up. Moses murdered an Egyptian but God transformed him into a leader. Peter denied the Lord but God transformed him into a powerful preacher. With persistence and patience, God seeks to remake us. Why? According to Paul, God gains a vessel of honor, sanctified, useful to the master, prepared for every good work (2 Tim. 2:20–21).

The human potter molds a clay container on a wheel and matures it in a kiln. Fire hardens the clay and illuminates the glaze or color. The heat turns the clay into a functional vessel.

Jeremiah did not mention a kiln, but Isaiah promises that God watches over us as fire transforms us into serviceable vessels. "When you pass through waters, I will be with you; and when you pass through the rivers, they will not sweep over you. When you walk through the fire, you will not be burned; the flames will not set you ablaze" (Isa. 43:2).

The potter's purpose eventually is to remove a cup, bowl, jar, or pitcher from the wheel. Having yielded to the potter's design and labor, the vessel becomes independent of the potter's hand. At this point, the analogy breaks down between a human potter and God, the Potter. We always want to feel the touch of God's hand. However, the time arrives when we must benefit from the preparatory stage that enabled us to internalize spiritual truths and become doers of the word. Trusting His vessels, the Lord looses us to become transformers in the community. As I am writing, I wonder, Is the Lord comfortable in setting me free in my town? Perhaps He feels as a Father like I did as a mother.

When our three children were babies, we introduced them to God through nature, songs, and Bible pictures and stories. We exposed them to settings where other Christians influenced their moldable minds. Through the toddler, preschool, and elementary years, we piled up on one of their beds at night and progressed through a series of Bible stories with practical applications. They giggled, dozed, kicked each other, interrupted with news items of their day, and gazed at the wall with a bored expression. Often I wondered, Are they learning anything about the Bible? Is the nightly ritual worth the trouble of having each one bathed and dressed for bed at a precise time for the less than calm family gathering? By the time the three outgrew the children's series, ministers of youth entered their lives stressing the value of a quiet time. Again I wondered, Are they listening?

Time passed. Three teenagers said goodnight and closed the doors to their private bedroom havens. One evening after they had retired, I attempted to distribute freshly folded clothes to their respective rooms. A serendipity awaited behind each door. Quietly opening Julie's door, I saw her reading the Bible. Backing away, I stepped across the hall to crack open Barton's door. He was reading the Bible. A few steps down the hall, I tried to keep Adam's door from creaking but he heard the sound and looked up from the passage he was reading in the Bible.

I buried my head in those folded clothes and softly sobbed, "Being confident of this, that he who began a good work in you will carry it on to completion until the day of Christ Jesus" (Phil. 1:6). "Fear not, for I have redeemed you; I have summoned you by name; you are mine. When you pass through the waters, I will be with you; and when you pass through the rivers, they will not sweep over you. When you walk through the fire, you will not be burned; the flames will not set you ablaze" (Isa. 43:1–2). "I will say to the north, 'Give them up!' and to the south, 'Do not hold them back.' Bring my sons from afar and my daughters from the ends of the earth— everyone who is called by my name, whom I created for my glory, whom I formed and made" (43:6–7).

Our kilns are the trials and adversities that refine and purify, enabling us to endure. James gives a realistic view of hardships: "Consider it pure joy, my brothers, whenever you face trials of many kinds, because you know that the testing of your faith develops perseverance. Perseverance must finish its work so that you may be mature and complete, not lacking anything" (James 1:2–4). Psalm 66:10 reminds us: "For you, O God, tested us; you refined us like silver."

The pressure of life's circumstances does not indicate God's disapproval. The pressure is His confidence in our potential. Only substances containing valuable metals are placed in the refiner's fire. "Blessed is the man who perseveres under trial, because when he has stood the test, he will receive the crown of life that God has promised to those who love him" (James 1:12).

Steam escapes from blow holes in the tops of kilns. In life's kiln when we feel defeat or stress, 1 Corinthians 10:13 encourages us that "God is faithful; he will not let you be tempted beyond what you can bear. But when you are tempted, he will also provide a way out so that you can stand up under it." Life's kilns transform clay pots into personalized, functional vessels. That night, when I saw my children reading from the Bible, I turned loose a little. I recognized God was in the process of molding my children to be less dependent on their parents and more dependent on Him. Yes, as parents, we will always be a presence in their lives, but they belong to the Potter. He transformed them and freed them to be useful vessels.

In the Far East a splendid silent celebration surrounds the opening of the kiln. As the potter removes vessels from the oven, he recognizes each one. He tenderly caresses the new forms as a father cuddles his newborn baby. The guests, invited by special invitation, quietly watch in honor of the potter as he examines his handiwork. The potter addresses and encourages the pieces to be faithful to their purposes: to serve, to be emptied, to be refilled. All the guests share the delight and pleasure of the potter.[5]

God, the Potter, celebrates the transformation of each vessel: "The Lord your God is with you, he is mighty to save. He will take great delight in you, he will quiet you with his love, he will rejoice over you with singing" (Zeph. 3:17).

Valuable Vessels

Transformation suggests a change in spiritual growth from a fledgling follower of Christ to a committed seeker. Yieldedness is necessary for transformation. To yield means giving up to a stronger force. Yield also means to fill a need, to give in return. I invite you to step into the lives of ten people: the prominent and powerful, a fiscal agent and a fisherman, outcast women at a well and on a wall, a king in the shepherd's field and a queen in the court, a reluctant prophet and a behind-the-scenes helper. These people yielded to God's transforming power. They filled a need in their time. They gave us examples to follow.

Welcome to the lives of valuable vessels!

CHAPTER 1

Abraham and Sarah

God planned to bless and redeem the world. He transplanted Abraham and Sarah from Mesopotamia to Canaan. Through transformations in their lives, Abraham and Sarah became "heirs together of the grace of life" (1 Peter 3:6–7 KJV).

 **God's Choice of Clay**
Foundations of many buildings and rubble of a ziggurat are the only evidences that Ur, Abraham's hometown, was once a thriving harbor city. Instead of being a vagrant wanderer, Abraham probably lived in a highly developed society. Citizens lived in cities with planned streets, avenues, and elaborate buildings. Drainage ditches controlled the swamps caused by the Euphrates River. The people enjoyed a complex system of writing, established laws, fine arts, and the best available medical attention. Two thousand years before the Roman Empire, the phalanx, a complex battle formation, protected the military.

17

Ur, a commercial center, was the crossroads of trade routes. God's providence placed Abraham in a spot where he could gain a world vision. Although living among residents who worshiped Nanna, the moon god of Ur, Terah's family (Terah was Abraham's father) had some knowledge of the true God.

Historians document an anti-Semitic movement in Mesopotamia around the time of Abraham. Perhaps fear of annihilation by the reigning dynasty caused Terah to leave Ur traveling toward Canaan. "Terah took his son Abram, his grandson Lot son of Haran, and his daughter-in-law Sarai, the wife of Abram, and together they set out from Ur of the Chaldeans to go to Canaan. But when they came to Haran, they settled there" (Gen. 11:31). Haran, an established city, was located on the trade route winding from Mesopotamia through Canaan, and down into Egypt.

Canaan was Abraham's destination. A land bridge between Egypt and Mesopotamia, Canaan's passageway was filled with world travelers. Mountains, sea, and desert isolated Canaan. Therefore the population, living to themselves, seemed less ambitious, cultured, and sophisticated than other parts of the world.

In Canaan, Abraham had the best of both worlds. Living away from the confusion of a busy society allowed Abraham to meditate and to listen to God speak. At the same time, he kept abreast of world events by talking with folks in the passing caravans.[6]

Abraham must have been an astute businessman. Throughout his life he presided over a prosperous household. One instance in Genesis 13:2 relates that "Abram had become very wealthy in livestock and in silver and gold." Other instances in his life show him as magnanimous when he gave Lot first choice of the land (Gen. 13:8–10), as decisive when he separated from Lot (13:8–9), as bold when he rescued Lot (14:1–16), as uncompromising when he refused rewards from Sodom's king (14:22–24), as compassionate when he prayed for Abimelech's childless home (20:17–18), and as respected among other leaders (Gen. 23).

Sarah, a loyal wife, shared the dangers of nomadic life and the dreams of Abraham. She must have been more influential in her home than the average woman of that time. Perhaps Abraham valued her independent streak. She spoke her mind to him in complaining about Hagar's haughty attitude. "Then Sarai said to Abram, 'You are responsible for the wrong I am suffering. I put my servant in your arms, and now that she knows she is pregnant, she despises me. May the Lord judge between you and me.'" Abraham responded that Sarah could make her own decision about Hagar. "'Your servant is in your hands,' Abram said, 'Do with her whatever you think best'" (Gen. 16:5–6).

In a time when servants performed domestic duties, Abraham depended on Sarah's culinary skill. He hurried to her instead of to the servant-cook with instructions to bake bread for his three guests (18:1–6). "So Abraham hurried into the tent to Sarah. 'Quick,' he said, 'get three seahs of fine flour and knead it and bake some bread'" (18:6).

Sarah's sense of humor mixed with nervousness is shown in her initial response to the news of impending motherhood. "So Sarah laughed to herself as she thought, 'After I am worn out and my master is old, will I now have this pleasure?'" (18:12).

Sarah's protection of Isaac's inheritance complicated by her jealousy of Hagar surfaced as she watched Isaac and Ishmael play. "But Sarah saw that the son whom Hagar the Egyptian had borne to Abraham was mocking, and she said to Abraham, 'Get rid of that slave woman and her son, for that slave woman's son will never share in the inheritance with my son Isaac'" (21:9–10). Contemptuously, Sarah refused to call Hagar and Ishmael by name. She referred to them as the slave girl and the son of this woman.

With God's consent, Abraham sadly sent Hagar and Ishmael from his tents. "The matter distressed Abraham greatly because it concerned his son. But God said to him, 'Do not be so distressed about the boy and your maidservant. Listen to whatever Sarah tells you, because it is through Isaac that your offspring will be reckoned. I will make the son of the maidservant into a nation also, because he is your offspring.' Early the next morning Abraham took some food and a skin of water and gave them to Hagar. He set them on her shoulders and then sent her off with the boy" (21:11–14).

Despite a nomadic lifestyle, Isaac evidently had a stable home life in the tents of a couple who loved each other. He had happy memories of his mother. When Abraham's servant brought Rebecca to Isaac, he took her "into the tent that his mother Sarah had lived in, and she became his wife. Isaac loved

Rebecca, and so he was comforted for the loss of his mother" (Gen. 24:67 TEV).

The Wheel of Circumstances

God saw potential in the clay of Abraham and Sarah. He placed them on the wheel of circumstances to mold them into useful vessels.

Pressure of the Wheel:
From Venturers to Vessels

In Haran God called Abraham to leave his homeland and his relatives in order to gain a nation, a blessing, an inheritance, and the opportunity to bless others. The first work of redemption was to separate a people.

The initial step in Abraham's transformation was a simultaneous threefold action. He heard God's call because of his sensitivity to divine intervention. "So Abram left, as the Lord had told him; and Lot went with him" (Gen. 12:4). Abraham believed God's promise and obeyed. "By faith Abraham, when called to go to a place he would later receive as an inheritance, obeyed and went, even though he did not know where he was going" (Heb. 11:8).

Pressure of the Wheel: Drought in Canaan

An unexpected adversity, a drought in Canaan, caused Abraham's faith to waver, and he went to Egypt. There he introduced Sarah, his wife, as his sister. He feared for his life if the pharaoh desired to add Sarah to his harem. The lie put God's promise in jeopardy. God intervened and used the pharaoh to chastise Abraham and to send him out of Egypt (Gen. 12:10–20). Abraham and Sarah had not learned that God provides in every situation.

Abraham's strongest trait was his faith in God's leadership. He could trust God in momentous plans like founding a nation, but he hesitated to trust in a drought. Strengths can be stumbling blocks. "So, if you think you are standing firm, be careful that you don't fall!" (1 Cor. 10:12). Strange inconsistencies are flaws in our lives. Abraham and Sarah's flaws were isolated failures, not the basic tenor of their lives. After they stumbled, they responded to God's re-molding.

Pressure of the Wheel: Ties of Kinship

Two instances involving Lot implied a flaw in Abraham's judgment. One instance was when the Lord told Abraham to leave his country and family. Abraham did leave, but Lot went with him (Gen. 12:1,4). The other instance was when "Abram went up from Egypt to the Negev, with his wife and everything he had, and Lot went with him" (13:1). The Lord's call included leaving relatives. For Abraham, an absolute break was difficult because of a natural tendency to enjoy family. Yet Lot did not share Abraham's call. Lot was materialistic, selfish, and worldly. Abraham had to abandon ties of kinship that would stifle his faith. God used Abraham's resoluteness to remove the flaw (Gen. 13). But Abraham never relinquished hope for Lot (Gen. 14).

Pressure of the Wheel: Plea for Sodom

Abraham's pleading intercession for Sodom is one of the most compassionate conversations in the Scriptures (Gen. 18:16–33). His audacious response to God's revelation of Sodom's judgment widens our eyes and causes gasps. He interceded with redemptive prayers for his family. When God judged Sodom and Gomorrah, He showed mercy toward Lot. "So when God destroyed the cities of the plain, he remembered Abraham, and he brought Lot out of the catastrophe that overthrew the cities where Lot had lived" (19:29).

Pressure of the Wheel: Sarah's Barrenness

Bearing a son was considered the most important duty of a woman to her husband. Barrenness was the tragedy of Sarah's life. When Isaac was born, Sarah was ecstatic for Abraham. "Who would have said to Abraham that Sarah would nurse children? Yet I have borne him a son in his old age" (Gen. 21:7).

However, before Isaac's birth, Sarah's flaw of impatience in waiting on God surfaced. Yielding to a legitimate custom, she gave Hagar, her handmaid, to Abraham as a surrogate mother (Gen. 16:1–4). To achieve spiritual ends through worldly means is dangerous. Remembering that God will not be hurried is an important lesson to learn. The promise of Sarah's giving birth in her old age was a problem for Abraham. After hearing God's announcement about blessing Sarah with a son, "Abraham fell face down; he laughed" in disbelief (17:17). Another flaw, that of jealousy, resulted in sending Hagar and Ishmael out of their tents to wander in the wilderness (21:9–21).

Pressure of the Wheel: Ishmael

At Sarah's suggestion, Abraham tried to force God's hand; Hagar became the mother of his son, Ishmael. From then on discord disturbed the peace of the home. A slave born into the home of a childless couple could inherit the estate. Abraham followed the custom of that day and asked, "Why not let Ishmael be my heir?" (Gen. 17:18 TEV). However, his request indicated he had not learned that God will provide.

Abraham always showed paternal affection for Ishmael even though Ishmael lived as "a wild donkey of a man; his hand will be against everyone and everyone's hand against him, and he will live in hostility toward all his brothers" (Gen. 16:12). Because of Abraham's request, God blessed Ishmael (17:20). "God was with the boy as he grew up. He lived in the desert and became an archer" (21:20).

Although Abraham had other sons by Keturah (25:1–2) after Sarah died, Isaac and Ishmael remained very close to their father. To me, a tender moment in the Bible is Genesis 25:7–9 (TEV): "Abraham died at the ripe old age of 175. His sons Isaac and Ishmael buried him in Machpelah Cave" with Sarah.

Pressure of the Wheel: Isaac

Through the pressures of life's circumstances, God often repeated His promise as an encouraging reminder for Abraham to keep striving. The long postponement between the promise of an heir and

Isaac's birth caused Abraham to ask, "Why?" God's response honed Abraham's faith that God could give him a child. The delay was an important resting stage for the clay.

Abraham's transformation culminated in his willingness to endure the supreme pressure—the sacrifice of Isaac. In his intercession for Sodom, Abraham had asked, "Will not the Judge of all the earth do right?" (Gen. 18:25) The trial Abraham faced would prove his belief in that truth. God's gradual molding enabled Abraham to relinquish his most cherished possession, his son of promise. God asked Abraham to sacrifice the only person who could fulfill the promise.

The pressures on the wheel taught him "obedient reverence for God" (Gen. 22:12 TEV) and Abraham "reckoned that God was able to raise Isaac from death" (Heb. 11:19 TEV). Abraham named the altar Jehovah-Jireh, the Lord provides.

When Abraham raised the knife over Isaac's body, God recognized His finished vessel through whom He could bless the world.

What We Learn About Transformation from Abraham and Sarah

- Transformation involves a sensitivity to hear, to trust, and to obey God's call.
- A wavering faith slows but does not stop the process of transformation.
- God provides resources and relationships to aid our transformation.

- Transformation occurs in stages through fresh revelations of God.
- One transformed person's obedience has possibilities to bless many people.
- Prayer adds undeniable strengths for transforming our clay vessels. In Genesis 11–25, I watched God mold venturers into vessels. I reflected on the prayers woven through the wheel's pressures, deepening faith and increasing trust. I learned from Abraham's conversational prayers that I can talk easily to God about His call and promises in my life. I can intercede with bold humility. I can pray knowing that God remembers our conversations. I can ask, Why? How? When?
- Worship adds strength for transforming clay vessels. Worship was paramount to Abraham. He built altars all over Canaan. In my imagination, I knelt beside each one and overheard Abraham:

"I felt His presence and heard Him say, 'Abraham, do as I say and I will bless you and make you a blessing.' You ask me, 'How did I leave all that was dear and familiar?' I accepted the relationship that Jehovah offered, and as I look back, I see that He took care of people every day. They were thrilling days, learning days. I walked among people bound by earth gods. Yet I was free. Let me tell you how this came to be:

"I laid on the altar my time. I found myself wanting to hurry through the days to reach the day when my son and heir would be born. I learned that Jehovah is in no hurry in working out His plans.

People fret and fume, and hurry and bustle about, but Jehovah has all eternity at his disposal. He works leisurely and with deliberation. God impressed me to turn my attention to the time we had together and to trust Him to take care of tomorrow. I became aware of an everlasting God.

"I laid on the altar my failures. In my weakest moments with the pharaoh in Egypt and Abimelech in Canaan, Jehovah intervened. All that Abimelech saw was a man guilty of deception. But Jehovah looked at me as a forgiven but wayward child. He spoke of me as a prophet and made Abimelech debtor to my prayers. I learned long afterwards in glory that Jehovah forgave and did not remember my sins: 'Therefore, there is now no condemnation for those who are in Christ Jesus' (Rom. 8:1) is an echo of the grace I knew. My failures became an opportunity to witness. Abimelech, the pagan ruler, exclaimed, 'God is with you in everything you do' (Gen. 21:22). I became aware of God's almightiness.

"I laid on the altar my livelihood. Jehovah prospered my herds and gave me a comfortable life, even one of prominence among my neighbors. I became aware of God's sovereignty.

"I laid on the altar my attitudes. I became concerned about that disreputable Lot and even prayed for his deliverance. I became concerned about Abimelech's childless home and Jehovah answered my plea about his family. My attitude could be firm with the king of Sodom who offered me rewards for helping in a battle. With the Lord as my shield, I could say, 'King of Sodom . . . I will accept nothing belonging to you, not even a thread or the thong of a sandal, so that you will never be able to say, "I made Abram rich"' (Gen. 14:22–23). I became aware of God's faithfulness.

"I laid on the altar my burdens. I felt the heart-break of sending my son, Ishmael, out from his home into the wilderness. I cried out to Jehovah and then laid down the burden. And Jehovah spoke, 'As for Ishmael, I have heard you: I will surely bless him; I will make him fruitful and will greatly increase his numbers. He will be the father of twelve rulers, and I will make him into a great nation' (Gen. 17:20). I became aware of God's grace.

"I laid on the altar my past, my present, and my future in the form of Isaac, my son. My son! 'For God so loved the world that he gave his one and only Son, that whoever believes in him shall not perish but have eternal life' (John 3:16). Through the agony of God, the Father, came the blessing for all of mankind that I had been promised.

"Bring to the altar your time, failures, abilities, at-titudes, your burdens, your willingness to turn loose all that is dear and allow Christ preeminence.

"We come to the altar of the same God, but have you noticed one vital difference? In the old covenant, God had to say, 'Abraham, do this, do that, go here, go there.' I had no example to pattern my life after. Because of the cross and the resurrection, God says to you, 'Follow me. I'll show you the way.'"

Questions to Consider

1. Describe the process in God's transformation of

Abraham and Sarah as mentioned in Genesis 18:19.

2. What did the actions of Abraham and Sarah reveal about their strengths and weaknesses?
3. If Abraham could have returned to Ur for a re-union with his peers, what experiences do you think he would have chosen to share?
4. What resources and relationships in your life indicate that the Lord provides for you?

If you could mold Abraham and Sarah, what kind of vessel would you fashion?

CHAPTER 2

Moses

God planned to lead the Hebrews out of slavery and into Canaan. He transformed an Egyptian prince and fiery Hebrew into a formidable deliverer of His people and delegator of laws.

God's Choice of Clay

Death in the Nile River awaited the birth of slave Jochebed's third child. A monstrous edict from the pharaoh that "every boy that is born you must throw into the Nile" brought terror to every Hebrew family (Ex. 1:22). However, God's providence in the choice of clay was evident. He turned Jochebed's grief into determination to save her son. "But when she could hide him no longer, she got a papyrus basket for him and coated it with tar and pitch. Then she placed the child in it and put it among the reeds along the bank of the Nile" (2:3). God prompted the princess who rescued Moses to hire Jochebed to nurse her own child (2:7–9). He impressed Moses with his Hebrew heritage through the influence and

31

fearless courage of his parents (Heb. 11:27).

In time, God's providence moved Moses from the slave hut of his parents to the splendor and privileges of the palace. The move was more than physical. Although the court lifestyle seemed an unlikely environment for God to prepare a future leader, certain aspects benefited Moses.

For example, "He was taught all the wisdom of the Egyptians and became a great man in words and deeds" (Acts 7:22 TEV). Moses was probably trilingual, able to read and write Hebrew, Egyptian hieroglyphs, and Babylonian cuneiform, the international and diplomatic language.[7] His ability to write enabled him to record the details of the wilderness wanderings (Deut. 31:24; Num. 33:2).

Ancient Egyptian educators required memorization of the classics. I encourage you to read each word of Exodus, Leviticus, Numbers, and Deuteronomy. Be amazed at the myriad details Moses had to interpret and explain to former slaves about altars, offerings, dimensions, laws, garments, instructions, directions, festivals, commandments, regulations, rules, duties, boundaries, and covenants. In Egypt God enrolled Moses in the memorization class. He educated a leader to receive in his mind the moral and spiritual laws on which to establish a civilization.

In Egypt Moses lived among the finest creative artists, skilled craftsmen, and fashion designers. So when God described how to build an "altar of acacia wood" (Ex. 27:1), to embroider a sash (28:4), and to engrave a precious stone (28:21), Moses was in his milieu. He understood that Jehovah was the God of the particulars.

Religiously Moses was a Hebrew. Culturally he was an Egyptian. When Zipporah explained to her father how the stranger, Moses, rescued her from harassing shepherds, she referred to him as "an Egyptian" (Ex. 2:19). I imagine Moses struggled with his identity. One day God impressed him to visit the slaves. Stephen related, "It came into his heart to visit his brethren" (Acts 7:23 KJV). On that visit, Moses killed an Egyptian who abused his kinsman. God began kneading out Moses' impulsive behavior that surfaced again at Sinai when he broke the tablets and at Kadesh when he struck the rock.

The Wheel of Circumstances
God saw the potential in Moses' clay. He placed Moses on the wheel of circumstances to mold him into a useful vessel.

Pressure of the Wheel:
Midian Desert
By identifying with the slaves, Moses exchanged power for the poverty and afflictions of the Hebrews. He fled to the desert to escape the consequences of murder. God weathered Moses' clay in the desert to keep him from breaking under stress. In the solitude, God began Moses' on-site leadership training.

In Midian, Moses met Jethro, a hospitable priest, who became Moses' mentor (Ex. 2) and father-in-law. Jethro nurtured Moses as his confidant and as a common-sense counselor. He advised Moses to appoint helpers to judge the people (Ex. 18). Perhaps because of Jethro's example, Moses nurtured Joshua (Deut. 1:38; 31:6–8; 34:9). God uses the gifts and talents of many people to shape His vessels.

In Midian, Moses learned to survive the desert's parched terrain and harsh climates. Shepherding sheep and goats, he memorized every trail leading from oasis to oasis. He learned practical facts such as a tamarisk tree could sweeten bitter water.[8]

Pressure of the Wheel: Burning Bush

God did not beat around the burning bush when he called Moses. Enter meditatively into Exodus 3. Watch Moses cautiously approach the burning bush, remove his shoes, and cover his face. Watch him listen as the Lord with succinct rapidity relates His desire to rescue the Israelites, repeat the covenant, reveal His name, and commission Moses. Imagine how Moses felt hearing God say, "Now I am sending you to the king of Egypt so that you can lead my people out of his country" (Ex. 3:10 TEV). The burning bush was an unforgettable sign to Moses. In his farewell address he mentioned "the goodwill of Him that dwelt in the bush" (Deut. 33:16 KJV).

We realize, as Moses did, that in God's presence a single moment can inspire transformation. Moses' call at the burning bush was potent enough to send him back to Egypt and lead the people to freedom.

An experience like a trial, a conviction, an urge to minister will occur in our ordinary routines. We recognize the moment as extraordinary. Memory of the moment energizes and gives direction throughout life. When faithfulness falters and energy wanes for the Lord's work, we can return to our burning bush experience.

My high school sorority usually held its spring dance in the upstairs ballroom at the country club. However, on one particular spring date, adults had engaged the ballroom. The manager relocated our dance to the patio around the pool.

The dance conflicted with a basketball awards banquet that my date was required to attend. Over an hour late, he called to suggest he would meet me at the club. Almost before my mother stopped the car, I jumped to the curb. Out of habit and in haste, I bounded up the stairs to the ballroom. As I burst through the door into the darkened room, I remembered that we were downstairs around the pool.

At that same instant, a man grabbed me and away we whirled across the floor. When my eyes grew accustomed to the dim light, I recognized my partner as the father of a friend. In fact, most of the adults were parents of teenagers I knew.

I shoved the man and ran to the lounge, followed by three of the women. They tried to soothe away my fright and embarrassment. When the women moved away, I saw my reflection in a wall of mirrors. I saw a teenager in a blue organdy gown and silver ballerina slippers. I thought, "My how this organdy itches. How uncomfortable I'll be dressed like this for the rest of my life. And with my interests and with my friends, I will be here for the rest of my life."

Gaining a measure of composure, I slowly started down the stairs one at a time. On each step I repeated, "There has to be a better way. There has to be a better way." At the foot of the stairs, a distinct impression branded my brain. "There is another way, in another direction."

I had ascended those stairs a carefree kid whose goal in life was to marry a successful man and spend my days in the country club. Thirty minutes changed all those plans. I descended the stairs realizing I did not know myself at all and that I was being tapped for something I did not understand.

Changing directions was not easy. Slowly a new way to live and a new way to walk evolved. Sometimes external pressures or internal stresses disorient my walk or cloud my sense of devotion. But I can return to a time and place when God impressed me with His direction for my life. My mind and soul return to the transforming moment at the foot of the stairs in the country club.

Pressure of the Wheel: Facing Inadequacies
Moses listened to the responsibilities inherent in his call. He pled lack of certain qualifications: prestige (Ex. 3:11), authority (4:1), eloquence (4:10), self-esteem (4:13), ability to succeed (5:23). God replaced each reservation with a divine resource. The plague contests with Pharaoh, crossing the Red Sea,

maintenance of life on the journey, victory over enemies, organization of more than 600,000 people, and even the good-bye at Canaan's border testify to God's unlimited power.

Verbalizing our inadequacies to the Lord aids in firming our transformation. We confront our weaknesses and commit them to His strength. We honor the Lord by recognizing that successful service is from His power, not from our human ingenuity.

Pressure of the Wheel: Test of Leadership

Moses grew up in the pharaoh's court but events, choices, and God's will caused him to oppose the pharaoh. Returning to Egypt to lead out the people was the first step toward fulfilling God's promise to give them the land of Canaan. During the plagues, compromise was a possibility in resolving the conflict with the pharaoh. However, Moses' single purpose of unconditional release of the Hebrews kept him focused. Exodus 8:25–27 is an example of Moses' resistance to compromise: "Then Pharaoh summoned Moses and Aaron and said, 'Go, sacrifice to your God here in the land.'

"But Moses said, 'That would not be right. The sacrifices we offer the Lord our God would be detestable to the Egyptians. And if we offer sacrifices that are detestable in their eyes, will they not stone us? We must take a three-day journey into the desert to offer sacrifices to the Lord our God, as he commands us.'"

After years of bondage, the people had resigned themselves to living in Egypt. Rekindling enthusiasm for a long journey toward a dim promise of the past was a formidable task. Moses convinced the elders that God was delivering them (Ex. 4:27–31).

Pressure of the Wheel: Relief for Moses
The pressure of the wheel wrenched a painful cry from Moses. "I cannot carry all these people by myself; the burden is too heavy for me" (Num. 11:14). The rabble among the masses groused and grumbled about the bland diet of manna (11:4). We can almost hear their whining. "Remember the fish we ate in Egypt at no cost—also the cucumbers, melons, leeks, onions and garlic. But now we have lost our appetite; we never see anything but this manna!" (11:5–6).

Dangling dangerously close to the end of his coping rope, Moses sought answers from God to valid questions. "He asked the Lord, 'Why have you brought this trouble on your servant? What have I done to displease you that you put the burden of all these people on me? Did I conceive all these people? Did I give them birth? Why do you tell me to carry them in my arms, as a nurse carries an infant, to the land you promised on oath to their forefathers? Where can I get meat for all these people? They keep wailing to me, "Give us meat to eat!" I cannot carry all these people by myself; the burden is too heavy for me'" (Num. 11:11–14).

Moses concluded that death was better than facing complaints that he considered a personal attack on his leadership (11:15).

The Lord's response gave Moses relief. He instructed Moses to choose 70 leaders and officials and to gather in the Tent of Meeting (11:16). The Lord anointed the leaders with the Spirit. He encouraged Moses with a promise of practical help. "They will help you carry the burden of the people so that you will not have to carry it alone" (11:17).

When you dangle close to the end of your coping rope, hurry to the Lord with the questions of Moses. "Why?" "What?" "Did I?" "Where?" Relief will come. Your vessel will glow with a glaze of intimate communication with God.

Pressure of the Wheel: Released

Moses did not begin the journey as a fully qualified vessel. He did begin it trusting in God's plan and desiring to obey. His transformation from an Egyptian prince and fiery Hebrew to a humble man (Num. 12:3) occurred on the journey through relationships, heartaches, worship, and prayer. Yet one experience when he presumed to be equal with God (20:12) excluded him from the Promised Land. We do not always see our hopes fulfilled on earth. Instead of sulking and complaining, Moses exulted in joy for the Israelites who did benefit from his labor. Moses, relying on God's wisdom, was content with a Mount Pisgah experience.

Our gracious God added a triumphant postscript by answering Moses' prayer, "Let me cross the Jordan River, Lord" (Deut. 3:25 TEV). Moses, along with Elijah, was there with Jesus at His Transfiguration. What a privilege! Moses crossed the Jordan River accompanied by our Lord.

 **What We Learn About Transformation from Moses**

- Changes required for a quality life take time. Moses spent 40 years in his solitary training. The discipline of waiting chafes, and we are tempted to take shortcuts. Moses' experience teaches that God's molding time is thorough and results in a useful vessel.

- Healthy secular influences can be additives to the clay of our lives. Moses' education was a definite plus for his particular kind of leadership. God's molding does not require that we live a cloistered existence. By waiting for a spectacular touch or an occurrence that zaps us with a transformation, we miss the minute changes in our preparation.

- Humility helps the Lord with our transformation. Humility is a tough, confident quality enabling us to stand firm in the face of foes. A humble person is teachable and willing to try when a service is needed. Humility means understanding our worth before God. Humility reins us back when we are tempted to react to the frustrations others cause us. Moses' life illustrates humility.

- Transformation involves voluntary choices. Moses' heredity and youthful environment were givens, but he could choose his life's direction. He weighed the pros and cons of his situation (Heb. 11:24–28). Outwardly he had nothing to gain by renouncing the privileges of the court and the pleasures of Egypt. Choosing to identify with the obscurity and afflictions of the slaves was a turning point in

Moses' life. Unless our choices coincide with God's purpose, all of life will be miserable.

- Moses chose the far view. He refused to let temporary treasures blind him to eternal wealth beginning on earth with usefulness and a godly character.

Questions to Consider

1. How did Moses' life in Egypt and in the Midian Desert prepare him to be a leader?
2. Are you surprised that Moses voiced inadequacies after his transformation at the burning bush? Why or why not? Why is depending on God's resources necessary to demonstrate our transformation?
3. What fact about Moses' transformation relates to you now?

If you could mold Moses, what kind of vessel would you fashion?

He kept his eyes on the future reward
(Heb. 11:26) TEV

Canaan

CHAPTER 3

Rahab

God planned to capture Jericho. He transformed a container stained by promiscuity into a helpful vessel.

God's Choice of Clay

If I were an artist, I would paint a picture of Jericho. Mudbrick houses nestled together along dirt streets. Dusty markets surrounded by the king's palace and Baal's temple. Flat-roofed houses clinging to the top of walls. I would paint the scene at late dusk coloring the city a dismal gray. On the west wall I would paint a house. From the window would dangle a cord, glinting crimson in the last ray of sun. I would title the picture *Safe*.

Rahab was a harlot and perhaps an innkeeper.[9] Stalks of flax drying on the flat roof hint that she might have been a weaver (Josh. 2:6). An unselfish, courageous risk taker, Rahab was susceptible to divine impressions. She showed devotion to her family as she included them in the escape plan from Jericho (6:23).

Although a Gentile, Rahab was knowledgeable of events in Hebrew history. From traveling merchants, she and other citizens heard about the Israelites' escape from Egypt and the miracles of their God. She discerned that the Israelites' God demonstrated greater power than the gods she worshiped.

Her reaction to the Israelites' nearby camp was different from the other Jericho citizens. Some of them despaired. Others felt smugly safe inside the walls of Jericho. After all, the nomads in the desert did not have military artillery. Still other citizens doubted that the Israelites could cross the rampaging Jordan River during the flood season. But Rahab realized the hand of a higher power directed the Hebrews.

The Wheel of Circumstances
God saw potential in Rahab's clay. He placed her on the wheel of circumstances to mold her into a useful vessel.

Pressure of the Wheel:
Arrival of the Spies
Moses had appointed Joshua as his successor. Joshua, a valiant soldier, led the Hebrews to conquer Canaan. Jericho was the barrier between Joshua and the future history of Israel. It was a key city to the Jordan valley. Before attacking Jericho, Joshua sent two skilled soldiers on a dangerous assignment to evaluate the strength and resistance of the city. Perhaps disguised as merchants, the spies entered Jericho and went to

Rahab's house. Perched on the wall, her house provided a panoramic view of the city. God's divine providence directed the spies to Rahab. He had impressed her to hide the men. God saw more in Rahab than the owner of a place to conceal spies. He saw latent possibilities for a future involving His own Son.

Rahab's reputation served as a cover because strangers regularly entered her residence. Because of the Israelite camp across the Jordan River, strangers in the town aroused suspicion. Perceiving they were observed coming into the city, Rahab hid the spies under flax on the roof. When the king dispatched guards to arrest the strangers, Rahab feigned ignorance of their identity and whereabouts. Disregarding personal risk, Rahab became God's servant! The pursuers, following Rahab's false directions, left the city to search for the spies. Rahab did not protect the spies because of pity or for her personal advantage. She discerned they were sent by their God.

Pressure of the Wheel: Saving Faith
Having protected the spies, Rahab returned to the roof. She believed the spies were men of God and willingly identified with them. She probably surprised the Hebrews by testifying to the strength of their God. She voiced a remarkable confession of faith, "I know that the Lord has given you this land" (Josh. 2:9 TEV). The words "has given" expressed her faith. She spoke of the future as if it had already been fulfilled. At that moment an Israelite victory seemed impossible. Yet Rahab regarded God's promise as already done. The initial step of faith justified her before God.

She also believed, "The Lord your God is God in heaven above and here on earth" (Josh. 2:11 TEV). Rahab's declaration is a remarkable arrow pointing toward Peter's confession, "You are the Christ" (Matt. 16:16). Rahab possessed little knowledge of spiritual truth. But she acted on what she knew. She did not wait until she understood all the law.

Pressure of the Wheel: Active Faith
Transformed, Rahab desired to help the spies. Rahab advised the spies about a safe route and about the caves honeycombed in the mountain in which to hide. She cautioned the men to stay in the caves for three days before returning to their camp. Then tying the cord around the waists of the spies, she lowered the men to the ground on the outside of the wall. The plan of action enabled them to escape without passing through the gates and risking capture. "She was put right with God through her actions, by welcoming the Israelite spies and by helping them to escape by a different road" (James 2:25 TEV). Rahab's faith inspired the deed (Heb. 11:31) and the deed expressed her faith (James 2:25–26). Faith is expensive. It benefits others.

Pressure of the Wheel: Safe
Trusting the word of the spies, Rahab made a covenant with them to save her and her family when the Hebrews attacked. She obeyed the instructions to hang a crimson cord in the window of her house. If she had refused to follow the spies' instruction or if she had thought the spies would remember her house on the wall, Rahab would have died as though she had never helped the

spies. Good deeds are worthless to save us. Only faith in God's mercy is essential for salvation.

From the window, she watched soldiers march in silence except for the blast on the ram's horn of the priest. She silently watched the defenders walk the wall. On the seventh day of battle, Jericho's walls tumbled. Rescuers, informed in advance, spirited Rahab and her family to safety. God honored Rahab's faith.

Our gracious God rewarded Rahab's faith by including her in the geneology of Jesus (Matt. 1:5). Rahab, the first convert to Judaism from a heathen religion, married Salmon, head of the tribe of Judah. Her child was Boaz, who married Ruth. Rahab's great-great-grandchild was David. Rahab's faith and repentance transformed a heathen harlot into an ancestor of Jesus.

What We Learn About Transformation from Rahab

- Trust in God is an essential first step in transformation.
- Transformation occurs in unlikely places.
- Complete understanding of spiritual truths is unnecessary for transformation. The transforming experience whets our interest to learn as much as possible about the mission and message of Christ.
- God's grace is sufficient to transform an immoral person into one of great faith. He sees latent possibilities for good when we see hopelessness. Rahab teaches us that God's crimson cord of love, patience, and mercy guarantees safety for anyone who in repentance reaches for the cord.

Because of Rahab's marriage to Salmon, we assume she joined the Hebrew camp. The Hebrews' encouragement of Rahab to remain faithful to the change in her life is a worthy example for us. Christians are often ready to pass judgment on new converts with immoral pasts. Because we all hold onto the same cord, we cannot in smug self-righteousness or haughty disdain point a finger at anyone. We are not good. We are forgiven.

Susie's Transformation

Susie, a probationer friend, lived in a rusty car, driven from bar to bar by her alcoholic mother. Sitting in a cloud of dirt and odors with an eye on the roaches, I looked at Susie's prized possession—a collection of photos of car wrecks she had survived. From that first hello, we honed a friendship. During Susie's teenage years, I tried to be a loving presence in her life. I watched her exist through multiple crises. My hope for her was slim.

As time passed, life situations moved us apart. Then in a note informing me of her marriage, Susie added, "My mother-in-law is a saved churchgoer." I thanked God for her Christian mother-in-law and continued to pray for Susie's salvation. Our letters decreased from spasmodic to hardly ever. Then one day, I cautiously slipped the letter opener into the envelope boldly marked, "Photos! Do Not Bend!" The handwriting had remained the same, although the return address had often changed through the years. I recognized a letter from Susie. She carefully captioned the photographs: "Me feeding the fawn." "Ducks at pond." "Me bathing Cloe—can you believe she is three?" "Vacation Bible School picnic at our pond. I teach toddlers."

When Jesus came to earth, He identified with all human experience. Thank you, Lord, for snatching people like Susie from a perilous existence to eternal life!

Questions to Consider

1. What kind of help did Rahab give to the spies? Why did she help them?
2. Read Hebrews 11:31, James 2:25, and Joshua 2:9. How do these verses relate to Rahab's transformation?
3. What fact about Rahab's transformation relates to your life now?

If you could mold Rahab, what kind of vessel would you fashion?

CHAPTER 4

David

God planned to establish a nation in Canaan. He transformed a shepherd seeking peaceful, safe pastures into a king who established peace and security for a nation (Psalm 78:70–72).

 **God's Choice of Clay**

David, son of Jesse from Bethlehem, "was ruddy, with a fine appearance and handsome features" (1 Sam. 16:12). Incidental references indicated an inharmonious home life. David may have been ignored by Jesse (16:11) and ridiculed by his brothers (17:28). Perhaps jealousy for having been passed over in favor of David caused the sibling rivalry. God saw within the young shepherd the bravery of a warrior, the articulation of a poet, the survival instinct of an exile, the nobility of a statesman, the sovereignty of a king, and a reverence for Jehovah.

David exemplified Paul's acknowledgment: "I do not understand what I do. For what I want to do I do not do, but what I hate I do" (Rom. 7:15). No doubt, the culture of harems, court intrigues, and avenging murders influenced David's mind-set and lifestyle. On the one hand he was faithful and devoted to God. On the other hand, he was ruthless and willing to commit heinous sins to satisfy his personal desires and ambitions. The Psalms mirror the satisfaction and the turmoil of his inner life.

David's complex personality exaggerated every event and situation. When you repeat David's name, what circumstances from his life form in your mind? His encounter with Goliath? Jonathan's friendship? Great kindness toward Mephibosheth, Jonathan's son? Derision of his religious enthusiasm by his wife, Michal? Pain of the rebellion and agony over the death of his son, Absalom? Desire to build a temple? Victorious battles? His self-restraint in regard to Saul? The trio: Bathsheba, Uriah, and Nathan?

Reading David's life without interruption reminded me of the expression, "Running off in all directions at the same time." But God cupped David's enormous energy in His hands and molded him into "a man after [His] own heart" (Acts 13:22).

The Wheel of Circumstances
God saw potential in David's clay. He placed David on the wheel of circumstances to mold him into a useful vessel.

Pressure of the Wheel: Adulation and Anxiety

After David's anointing by Samuel, he returned to his sheep with a new destiny. In isolation, David waited and honed skills used for his public appearances. He learned to play the lyre. This talent introduced him to Saul. The king engaged David to soothe his melancholy with music. David mastered the sling as a lethal weapon to rescue sheep from marauding animals. This ability enabled him to rescue the Israelite army from the Philistine, Goliath.

Successful in all his military missions, David became a national hero. Saul's animosity increased proportionately to David's public praise. The king became David's permanent enemy. "Saul became still more afraid of him, and he remained his enemy the rest of his days" (1 Sam. 18:29). With no hope of reconciliation David fled and eluded Saul's relentless pursuit for several years. David's words to Jonathan, "I am only a step away from death" (1 Sam. 20:3 TEV), describe his life of danger, apprehension, and rejection.

Joined by society's misfits, David eked out an existence, hid in caves, and lived with his enemies, the Philistines. He gained on-site training of the Philistines' strengths and weaknesses. Consequently, "in the course of time, David defeated the Philistines and subdued them" (2 Sam. 8:1).

Pressure of the Wheel: Rest for the Clay

The occasions David enjoyed with Jonathan were

rest for the clay. Perhaps Jonathan was the most stabilizing influence in David's life. To be a best friend to your worst enemy's son was the type of relationship that David could manage. Probably sharing a similar rash streak encouraged their friendship. Check out 1 Samuel 14.

Regardless of the friction between David and Saul, "Jonathan became one in the spirit with David, and he loved him as himself" (1 Sam. 18:1). First Samuel 20 describes the depth of Jonathan and David's friendship. Jonathan executed an elaborate plan to inform David of Saul's intention. The news was sad and Jonathan understood that his friend must flee for his life. They met in the woods and "David got up from the south side of the stone and bowed down before Jonathan three times, with his face to the ground. Then they kissed each other and wept together—but David wept the most. Jonathan said to David, 'Go in peace, for we have sworn friendship with each other in the name of the Lord, saying, "The Lord is witness between you and me, and between your descendants and my descendants forever."' Then David left, and Jonathan went back to the town" (20:41–42).

Later, learning of Jonathan's death, David "mourned and wept and fasted till evening for Saul and for his son Jonathan" (2 Sam. 1:12). David's lament in 2 Samuel 1:17–27 for Saul and Jonathan is one of the most emotional passages in the Bible. David concludes the eulogy, "I grieve for you, Jonathan my brother; you were very dear to me.

Your love for me was wonderful, more wonderful than that of a woman" (1:26).

David's grief produced a positive result. Much later he asked, "Is there anyone still left of the house of Saul to whom I can show kindness for Jonathan's sake?" (9:1). From a servant, he learned about Mephibosheth, Jonathan's son. When the child was five, he sustained a crippling fall. His physical challenge was probably not as devastating as his emotional one. Mephibosheth referred to himself as "a dead dog" (9:8). David sent for the boy and said, "Don't be afraid . . . for I will surely show you kindness for the sake of your father Jonathan. I will restore to you all the land that belonged to your grandfather Saul, and you will always eat at my table" (9:7). David gave the servant, Ziba, further instructions: "Then the king summoned Ziba, Saul's servant, and said to him, 'I have given your master's grandson everything that belonged to Saul and his family. You and your sons and your servants are to farm the land for him and bring in the crops, so that your master's grandson may be provided for. And Mephibosheth, grandson of your master, will always eat at my table'" (9:9–10).

"So Mephibosheth ate at David's table like one of the king's sons" (9:11) and appreciated the protection of David for the remainder of his life. We know David as a conqueror and a ruler, but this slice in his life shows King David being a foster father as best as he was able under unusual circumstances.

To endure the pressures of the wheel, God is good to give us friends who encourage, warn, comfort, and advise; who sit beside us and listen; and who sob with us through joy and sadness. All of us need someone with whom we are one in the spirit.

Pressure of the Wheel: Prosperous King

When David consolidated Israel and Judah, he "realized that the Lord had established him as king of Israel and was making his kingdom prosperous for the sake of his people" (2 Sam. 5:12 TEV). David turned his attention to conquering enemies (1 Chron. 18–20), returning the ark of the covenant to Jerusalem (15–16), organizing the kingdom (22–27), and making preparations to build the Temple (29:1–9).

Pressure of the Wheel: Spiritual Prayer

Busy being king, David neglected his relationship with God. Perhaps resting from his many kingly responsibilities, David stayed in Jerusalem during the seize of Rabbah. In an idle hour, he insisted on the company of his neighbor, Bathsheba. Pregnancy resulted from their affair. David tried to save himself from exposure by a cover-up scheme. He called Uriah, Bathsheba's husband, home from the war. Unable to entrap Uriah, who was loyal to the king, David wickedly plotted Uriah's death in battle. When David received the message of Uriah's death, his callous response was, "Say this to Joab: 'Don't let this upset you; the sword devours one as well as another'" (2 Sam. 11:25).

Pressure of the Wheel: David's Transformation

God abhorred David's arrogance, adultery, deception, and murder. So He sent Nathan to rebuke the
king. Appealing to David's sense of justice and
pity, the prophet asked David to pass judgment on
the parable of the lamb (2 Sam. 12:1–4).

When David expressed indignation at the selfish rich man for killing the sheep of the poor man,
he denounced himself. On hearing the penalties
for his sin, David did not resent Nathan nor argue
with him. He did not make excuses or denials. In
simple words expressing heartfelt feeling, he confessed, "I have sinned against the Lord" (12:13).

David's admission of guilt transformed a phi-
landering monarch into a penitent sinner. David
genuinely repented, and God immediately forgave.
Although forgiven, David lived with the inevitable
consequences of his sins.

From the Psalms we learn David desired that
the story of his fall, repentance, and God's forgiveness would "teach transgressors [God's] ways"
(Psalm 51:13). David did not fear losing the
throne, his life, or pleasures. But fearing he might
lose the presence of God, David pled, "Do not cast
me from your presence or take your Holy Spirit
from me" (51:11). More than any person or possession, David treasured God's friendship.

Pressure of the Wheel: A Summary

The wheel of circumstances turned through many

years from David's anointing until "he died at a good old age, having enjoyed long life, wealth and honor" (1 Chron. 29:28). David developed a buoyant reaction and resilient attitude toward life's circumstances (2 Sam. 12:21–23). One example is 2 Samuel 12:14–23. David's first child by Bathsheba became ill. David pled with God. He fasted. He refused comfort from the servants. When the child died, the servants feared telling David. "He may do something desperate, they whispered among themselves" (12:18). Learning of the baby's death, "David got up from the ground. After he had washed, put on lotions and changed his clothes, he went into the house of the Lord and worshiped. Then he went to his own house, and at his request they served him food, and he ate.

"His servants asked him, 'Why are you acting this way? While the child was alive, you fasted and wept, but now that the child is dead, you get up and eat!'

"He answered, 'While the child was still alive, I fasted and wept. I thought, "Who knows? The Lord may be gracious to me and let the child live." But now that he is dead, why should I fast? Can I bring him back again? I will go to him, but he will not return to me'" (2 Sam. 12:20–23).

David developed a dependence on God as he questioned, listened, and followed God's direction. Two examples are found in 1 Samuel: (1) "He inquired of the Lord, saying, 'Shall I go and attack these Philistines?'" (23:2); and (2) "David inquired of the Lord, 'Shall I pursue this raiding party? Will

I overtake them?' 'Pursue them,' he answered. 'You will certainly overtake them and succeed in the rescue'" (30:8). Above all, David revered Jehovah. In his most noble accomplishments and most base disappointments, his reverence for God remained.

What We Learn About Transformation from David

- Ideal circumstances are not pre-requisites for transformation. In fact, God can use the most unlikely person, situation, or event to change us. Transformation occurs in the mainstream of living or in our normal routines.
- God began where David was to shape him into a versatile vessel. God, the Potter, does not perfect a vessel and then decide its use. At our birth, He has our life plan in His mind. God's plan for David guided Samuel to eliminate seven of Jesse's sons as king candidates. "He chose David his servant and took him from the sheep pens; from tending the sheep he brought him to be the shepherd of his people Jacob, of Israel his inheritance" (Psalm 78:70–71). From the moment of his anointing, David's life was in process of becoming the vessel that God intended.
- Waiting is important for transformation. David's clay rested after his anointing and during his fugitive years.
- Inherent in our transformation is a warning. The changes that occur challenge us to more faithful

service which make us a mark for Satan. We must be alert to his devious schemes. We must be on guard to dodge the accurate aim of his obstacles. In a second, we stumble. David did. He had received God's mercy and forgiveness. But his transformation did not insulate him from Satan. Pride and lack of trust in God crept into his thinking. He took a census of those eligible to fight. The census moved the nation away from Moses' tradition toward a secular monarchy similar to the surrounding nations. David failed to trust God to win the battles. He robbed God of His glory.

Conscience-stricken David confessed, "O Lord, I beg you, take away the guilt of your servant. I have done a very foolish thing" (2 Sam. 24:10). At the threshing floor altar, God accepted the sacrifice, removed the plague from the people, and forgave David (24:18–25).

Questions to Consider

1. Schedule a time to read the events in 1 Samuel 16 through 1 Chronicles 29. Using a concordance, locate the Psalms David wrote describing some of the events. For example, Psalm 68 may be based on the return of the ark to Jerusalem recorded in 1 Chronicles 15. How does a study of the Psalms affect your feelings about David's behavior and attitudes?
2. Describe how God stretched David to produce high and low experiences in his life.

3. Describe how one fact about David's transformation relates to your life.

If you could mold David, what kind of vessel would you fashion?

CHAPTER 5

Esther

God planned to save the Jews from annihilation. He transformed an obscure, beautiful young woman into a strong advocate for her people.

God's Choice of Clay

Orphaned as a child, Esther had a tender affection for Mordecai, her cousin and adopted father. As an adult, "she continued to follow Mordecai's instructions as she had done when he was bringing her up" (Esther 2:20).

Devout Israelites, Mordecai's family had chosen to stay in Persia when Cyrus permitted the Jews to return to Palestine. Consequently, a generation had grown up without personal knowledge of that country. The Persian rulers tolerated various religious traditions and customs of the nations they conquered, and so Esther grew up observing the Sabbath and festivals, and hearing about the triumphs and tribulations of her ancestors. She worshiped Jehovah never suspecting a persecution like her ancestors had suffered, never suspecting her beauty would fit into God's purpose to avert a massacre of her race. Yet God saw potential for prudence and decisive courage in her stunning, spirited personality.

The Wheel of Circumstance

God saw potential in Esther's clay. He placed Esther on the wheel of circumstances to mold her into a useful vessel.

Pressure of the Wheel: Inside the Persian Palace

In the palace, Vashti, an honorable queen of King Xerxes, refused to humiliate herself before the king's drunken guests. Infuriated, the king banished Vashti and organized a beauty pageant to select a new consort. Esther, representing her province, moved into the harem with other hopeful girls. For one year they received a special beauty treatment.

Hegai, the administrator of the harem, favored Esther. He planned her beauty regimen and provided special food for Esther to eat. Hegai personally prepared Esther to meet King Xerxes. "Lovely in form and features" (Esther 2:7), she pleased Xerxes, who crowned her queen. In honor of Esther, the king "proclaimed a holiday throughout the provinces and distributed gifts with royal liberality" (2:18). Advised by Mordecai, Esther remained silent about her Jewish identity (2:20). With Esther poised in place on the wheel, God began molding her through events of divine providence.

Pressure of the Wheel: Massacre Plot

Mordecai refused to bow before Haman, the powerful prime minister with unlimited access to the king. Enraged by Mordecai's insult, Haman sought revenge on all Jews. Combining flattery with bribery, Haman explained to King Xerxes that Jews were troublemakers refusing to keep Persian laws. Haman suggested that by annihilating the Jews, the king could obtain all their wealth. Refusing the bribe, Xerxes assented to the mass murder.

With the king's permission, a day was set for the Jewish massacre. To add a personal touch, Haman built a gallows on which to hang Mordecai.

Couriers carried the decree to all the provinces. They posted the edict on the news columns in the town squares where residents learned of the approaching terrors. As the couriers continued on the relay circuit, the screams of the Jews mounted to a cacophonous mourn.

Esther's servants reported Mordecai's anguish. Deeply disturbed, Esther read the proclamation disclosing the wicked plot. She received Mordecai's message to plead with the king for mercy (Esther 4:1–8).

Pressure of the Wheel: Transformation

Esther had enjoyed preferential life in the palace. She hesitated when Mordecai asked her to intervene. Her indecision revealed a flaw. She wavered at the prospect of revealing her Jewish ethnicity. To protect the king from assassins, every visitor to the throne room had to be announced; therefore, Esther risked death appearing unannounced before the monarch. She was not particularly willing to sacrifice her life. Mordecai warned that her own life was at stake: "Do not think that because you are in the king's house you alone of all Jews will escape. For if you remain silent at this time, relief and deliverance for the Jews will arise from another place, but you and your father's family will perish. And who knows but that you have come to royal position for such a time as this?" (Esther 4:13–14). Mordecai challenged Esther to face this dilemma as the reason for her being queen. The heat from the kiln in Esther's life burned away her excuses and left her with a firm determination to help her people.

Encouraged by the prayers of her people, Esther understood that God had called her to a specific task. She accepted that her position brought responsibility. Entering the corridor connecting the harem with the audience hall, Esther passed representatives of the world waiting to see Xerxes. She passed his advisors and through the embroidered curtain into the inner court. Xerxes raised his golden scepter to welcome Esther. He promised her her heart's desire.

God used Esther's willingness to sacrifice herself to set in motion events that saved His people. Esther developed a plan to expose Haman as the villain. Although she had the confidence of her husband, she moved with slow discretion. Esther invited Xerxes and Haman to a banquet, but she refused to state her heart's desire. God's hand delayed the process. On that night because of insomnia, the king read the royal chronicles. He learned that Mordecai had not been honored for uncovering a plot to assassinate the king (Esther 2:21–23; 6:1–3). The next morning, Haman came to talk about the executions. But Xerxes asked advice for how to honor a man. Haman assumed the king referred to him. So he suggested dressing the man in royal robes to ride on a horse with a royal crest. In addition, a nobleman must lead the honoree through the streets proclaiming, "This is what is done for the man the king delights to honor" (6:9).

To Haman's horror, the king ordered him to administer all the honors to Mordecai (Esther 6). Mordecai's reward continued through the years. "He was honored and well-liked by His fellow Jews. He worked for the good of his people and for the security of all their descendants" (Esther 10:3 TEV).

Esther invited Xerxes and Haman to a second banquet. She revealed Haman's plot to exterminate the Jews. The enraged king hanged Haman on the gallows built for Mordecai. With Esther's urging, the king issued a counter order empowering Jews to defend themselves. Esther was instrumental in seeking permanent protection for the Jews.

What We Learn About Transformation from Esther

- God uses people to help us experience transformation. God cultivated a relationship between Mordecai and Esther. In God's providence, He used Mordecai to interpret to Esther her reason for being queen.

During a study of juvenile delinquency in a Round Table group, I developed a keen interest for youth in lifestyles different from mine. Mr. Osborne, the chief probation officer, interpreted the unusual compassion as God's way of directing me toward a ministry. Mr. Osborne offered the ministry as a volunteer in his court. God led me to a person who could interpret His plan for my life. God used a secular organization to set in motion a series of events that allow me to share with you now.

- God uses seemingly trivial or ordinary incidents as pivots for His transforming purposes. A beauty pageant brought Esther into prominence enabling her to save her people. Insomnia caused Xerxes to learn of Mordecai's service just in time to spare his life (Esther 6:4).

No experience is wasted with God. Your pleasant or unpleasant situation is preparing you for a future event or relationship. My experience has been that present situations link to future ones. For example, during a re-treat, I praise God for the inspiration, the learning, and the friendships of the moment. At the same time I know that something I am seeing, hearing, or someone I am meeting will be a part of the future. Even as I participate with enthusiasm, I realize the duality of the moment.

On one occasion, in a seminar, I listened to a speaker discuss change. She stood near a door marked Exit. With my eyes riveted on the sign and my mind listening to words, I repeatedly interchanged: exit-change, change-exit. Months later I received an invitation to lead a retreat about change. *Exit* came to mind. I decided the theme should be *Exits We Make in Life.* A trivial word, ingrained in my thoughts, developed a retreat theme.

Questions to Consider

1. What personality strengths did God see in Esther?
2. What events in Esther's life would non-Christians call coincidences and Christians call providence?
3. Using anecdotes from Esther's life, illustrate Mordecai's challenge, "And who knows but that you have come to the royal position for such a time as this" (Esther 4:14).

If you could mold Esther, what kind of vessel would you fashion?

CHAPTER 6

Jonah

God's plan was to save Nineveh. He transformed a resistant prophet with an attitude problem into an evangelist.

God's Choice of Clay

Jonah, a prophet, lived in Galilee. He knew God as loving, merciful, and patient (Jonah 4:2). Yet stubbornness, prejudice, and self-pity characterized his own personality. A narrow-minded nationalism caused him to like some people and dislike others.

In Jonah's day Nineveh was the worst of Israel's enemies. At the height of its power, atrocities, and splendor, Nineveh was the capital of the Assyrian empire. Patriotic Jews hated "the bloody city . . . full of lies and robbery" (Nah. 3:1 NKJV). No doubt, Jonah shared their feelings. Warrior kings exterminated entire populations of conquered cities. Most prophets pronounced judgment on heathen nations from long distance instead of traveling to the places to preach. Jonah resented God's universal love and rebelled against his duty when God commissioned him to go to Nineveh (Jonah 1:2). After all, the Assyrians had enslaved his fellow Jews, and his honor was at stake if God should forgive them.

The Wheel of Circumstances
God saw potential in Jonah's clay. He placed Jonah on the wheel of circumstances to mold him into a useful vessel.

Pressure of the Wheel: Jonah's Disobedience
To evade God's unexpected call and to run away from the Lord, Jonah boarded a ship at Joppa bound for Tarshish, Spain. The ship's destination was the opposite direction from Nineveh. Being a prophet, to disobey God's command caused discomfort. And so, Jonah tried to go as far away as possible from any reminder of God.

The Lord hurled a violent wind on the sea causing the ship to toss like a cork. The ship was at the mercy of the wind and the waves as described in Psalm 107:25–27: "For he spoke and stirred up a tempest that lifted high the waves. They mounted up to the heavens and went down to the depths; in their peril their courage melted away. They reeled and staggered like drunken men; They were at their wits' end."

Not too uncomfortable or uneasy to sleep, Jonah snoozed during the pandemonium. The mariners cast cargo into the sea and prayed to their gods to quell the raging waves. Neither their prayers nor their navigation skills controlled the ship.

The captain, remembering Jonah, shook him awake and inquired, "How can you sleep? Get up and call on your god! Maybe he will take notice of us, and we will not perish" (Jonah 1:6). A trial by casting lots determined that Jonah's presence precipitated the storm. Jonah discovered the truth of Psalm 139:7: "Where can I go from your Spirit? Where can I flee from your presence?"

Pressure of the Wheel: Jonah's Transformation

The captain desperately rebuked Jonah with many questions: "Tell us, who is responsible for making all this trouble for us? What do you do? Where do you come from? What is your country? From what people are you?" (Jonah 1:8). The questions were natural inquiries but asking about Jonah's occupation must have pierced his heart. Jonah's response was an appropriate résumé answer: "I am a Hebrew and I worship the Lord, the God of heaven, who made the sea and the land" (1:9). Actually, the pagan sailors seemed more in awe of Jonah's God than Jonah seemed to be. Terrified, they asked him how to calm the sea. Jonah faced the consequences of his disobedience and admitted he must be sacrificed.

The mariners were unwilling to condemn Jonah without hearing his defense. So Jonah confessed to his rebellion against His Lord's will that imperiled the sailors. He repented and accepted the penalty. Jonah's willingness to sacrifice himself for the sailors' safety evidenced a sense of justice as well as a spiritual regeneration. No one sins to himself. Jonah's sin touched the lives of strangers. Repentance motivates a concern for people we hurt. Touched by Jonah's confession and proposal, the sailors cried out to God for forgiveness as they tossed Jonah into the sea. The storm ceased.

Thrown overboard, Jonah was rescued by a fish. Jonah admitted his helplessness, his hope, and his revelation that God loves the world. Inside the fish, God crushed the clay. Jonah had known theoretically about God's judgment. But the sea experience taught him firsthand about God's judgment. In a situation beyond his control, Jonah praised God for hearing and answering prayer, for His protection, for another chance to worship in the temple, and for another opportunity to preach (Jonah 2).

Jonah's experience—"When my life was ebbing away, I remembered you, Lord" (2:7)—is comforting to me. Think about your death. Your last conscious thought remembering Jesus serenely merges into the reality of His presence.

By the time he reached Nineveh, Jonah could preach convincingly about judgment. He promised to preach salvation to "those who worship worthless idols" (2:7–9 TEV). God knew that Jonah was ready to preach. God's graciousness gave Jonah a second chance.

Pressure of the Wheel: Revival

God crushed Jonah's clay with merciful hands. He remolded a grudgingly obedient vessel. Jonah's heart did not accept God's purpose, but he could not escape God's call.

No doubt, Jonah's presence and proclamation caught the attention of the Ninevites. His austere dress and manner contrasted with the pomp and luxury of the city. The terse, repetitious prediction of destruction caused an unusual reaction to sweep through Nineveh. In this instance, God's mercy was expressed toward Nineveh. He gave them 40 days to repent. From beggars to the king, all people responded overwhelmingly. They prayed, dressed in sackcloth, and humbled themselves before God. They repented of their wicked behavior and evil actions (Jonah 3:5).

When the king heard the message, he issued a decree: "Do not let any man or beast, herd or flock, taste anything; do not let them eat or drink. But let man and beast be covered with sackcloth. Let everyone call urgently on God. Let them give up their evil ways and their violence. Who knows? God may yet relent and with compassion turn from his fierce anger so that we will not perish" (3:7–9).

When Jesus faced unbelief from the people, He recalled Jonah's revival: "The men of Nineveh will stand up at the judgment with this generation and condemn it; for they repented at the preaching of Jonah, and now one greater than Jonah is here" (Luke 11:32). Jesus referred to himself as a sign of Jonah: "For as Jonah was a sign to the Ninevites, so

also will the Son of Man be to this generation"
(11:30). Jesus honored Jonah by singling out his
preaching as the most powerful and successful until the time of Jesus (Matt. 12:41).

Pressure of the Wheel: God's Rebuke

Success in his ministry enraged Jonah. Sarcastically,
he questioned the Potter about saving Nineveh: "O
Lord, is this not what I said when I was still at home?
That is why I was so quick to flee to Tarshish. I knew
that you are a gracious and compassionate God,
slow to anger and abounding in love, a God who re-
lents from sending calamity" (Jonah 4:2). Jonah
wanted to limit God's mercy.

Jonah was a powerful preacher but a personal
failure. Instead of weeping with joy and worshiping
with new converts, he went out east of the city to
watch the people's reaction to his preaching. While
Jonah sulks, think about how an unexpected turn of
events or change in relationships may be undesired.
How do you react to a failure, a disappointment, a
handicap, a demotion or a promotion of another, a
death, a rejection, a denied dream?

Joseph reacted to unexpected events differently
than Jonah. Joseph's life was routine until being
kidnapped and sold into slavery by his own
brothers. From then on, Joseph lived through
many unwanted experiences. Refusing to be bitter,
Joseph grew in kindness, integrity, humility, and
wisdom. Talking to his brothers, he expressed his
philosophy, "You intended to harm me, but God
intended it for good to accomplish what is now

being done, the saving of many lives" (Gen. 50:20).

The wheel of circumstances has no control over you unless you let it. The outcome of relationships and situations depends on an inner quality of life. What happens to us is not as important as how we react to the happening. Aren't we thankful for our God Who mercifully molds us through unexpected experiences of life?

Let's return to Jonah. To ease Jonah's discomfort, God caused a vine to grow giving Jonah shade. Happy about the vine, Jonah still hated the Ninevites. At dawn the sun, the wind, and a worm withered the vine. Jonah threw a fit.

God shamed Jonah's prejudice and showed the absurdity of his attitude by contrasting their feelings. Jonah felt pity for the wilted plant that he did not make grow. God felt love for 120,000 individuals whom He created (Jonah 4:10–11). Jonah ignored the sunrise conversation with God. His last words to us complain of the heat and grumble about his rights (4:8–9).

What We Learn About Transformation from Jonah

- Transformation does not mean perfection. God used the words of His prejudiced prophet to convict the Ninevites of their sin.
- Jonah's gift of preaching revived a city because his gift had spiritual worth, even though functioning through an imperfect life. The use of gifts

does not assure that love is the motive. Paul reminds us that without love, the gifted person is nothing (1 Cor. 13:2). Jonah illustrated Paul's observation. His experience cautions us to examine our motives for service.

- We need to be prepared for an increase in negative personal reaction due to transformation. How often do we go through the motions of speaking or serving but our hearts are indifferent, maybe even cold?

Questions to Consider

1. Why did Jonah run away in response to God's call? Have you ever evaded God's call? If so, how?

2. Read Jonah's prayer in 2:1–9. How is it a prayer of thanksgiving, a call for help, and a promise of commitment?

3. How do you feel about Jonah's response to the revival? Do you ever limit God's mercy to yourself or to others?

If you could mold Jonah, what kind of vessel would you fashion?

I have every right to be angry—angry enough to die
(Jonah 4:9 TEV)

CHAPTER 7

Andrew

God planned to introduce Jesus to the people. He took a quiet fisherman and changed him into a consistent helper and witness.

 **God's Choice of Clay**
Opening the Gospels, we almost hear Peter declaring his love for Jesus, splashing in the Sea of Galilee, sobbing in the courtyard, and preaching at Pentecost. Looking past Peter, we see his brother, Andrew, chatting with a child about his lunch or welcoming some Greeks. Brothers differ in their personalities. Perhaps as children, Peter was aggressive and flamboyant; Andrew, more subdued. Andrew understood Peter's instinctive leadership abilities. He never seemed resentful being identified as Peter's brother. His temperament made him content to blend into the background.

Although not flashy, Andrew was not a loner. On at least one occasion, he joined the inner circle—Peter, James, and John—to ask Jesus questions about things to come (Mark 13:3). He frequently prayed with the disciples and the women. He was present to vote on Judas's successor (Acts 1:13–26).

The Wheel of Circumstances
God saw potential in Andrew's clay. He placed Andrew on the wheel of circumstances to mold him into a useful vessel.

Pressure of the Wheel: John the Baptist's Message
John the Baptist was an effective teacher for Andrew. As a follower of John the Baptist, Andrew heard him when he "preached the Good News to the people and urged them to change their ways" (Luke 3:18 TEV). Perhaps Andrew confessed his sins and was baptized by John. He probably stood on Jordan's banks overhearing John's scathing sermon to the Pharisees and Sadducees (3:7–9). He heard John answer the questions of individuals in the crowd (3:10–14).

Pressure of the Wheel: Andrew's Transformation
About four o'clock one afternoon (John 1:39), Andrew and John, the fishermen, stood with John the Baptist on the east side of the Jordan River (1:28). Jesus walked by and John the Baptist exclaimed, "Look, the Lamb of God!" (1:35). Immediately Andrew and John followed Jesus Who asked them, "What do you want?" (1:38). Probably at

that point the men were dubious about what they wanted. They stammered a question about Jesus' residence. At Jesus' invitation, Andrew and John spent the day with Him.

The unrecorded conversation may have been similar to Jesus' discourse with the two men from Emmaus. If so, Andrew experienced a fire burning within him as Jesus explained the Scriptures (Luke 24:32). Whatever happened convinced Andrew that Jesus was the Messiah. The memorable afternoon spent with Jesus transformed Andrew into a consistent helper and witness.

Within a few days, Jesus called the first of His disciples including Andrew. The discipline and instruction of Jesus on a daily basis motivated Andrew to remain faithful throughout his life. Tradition places Andrew as a preacher among the Scythians who were "rough, uncouth, and savage." Tradition adds that Andrew was martyred—bound not nailed—to an X-shaped cross. He died of hunger, thirst, and exposure.[10]

Pressure of the Wheel: A Willing Witness

"We have found the Messiah" (John 1:41) became a life-theme for Andrew. Every time Andrew appears in the Gospels, he is bringing someone to Jesus. God used Andrew to introduce Peter to Jesus. I imagine Peter was in the vicinity of the lake mending nets on the shore or preparing to sail. Immediately after leaving Jesus, Andrew rushed to the lake. Some distance from Peter, he cupped his hands to his mouth like a megaphone shouting, "We've found the Messiah!"

Understanding Peter's personality, Andrew knew better than to shout an uncertain belief like, "Maybe we've found the Messiah," or "I think I met the Messiah." Peter never would have acknowledged anything less than a decisive conviction.

To speak to a brother about the Lord often takes more courage and faith than to speak to a stranger. Our life and character will mock, cancel, or enhance our testimony. Nothing awkward in their relationship interfered with Andrew's testimony. Since they shared a home in Bethsaida, the brothers knew the best and the worst about each other (John 1:44).

Pressure of the Wheel: Willing Helper
God used Andrew to introduce a boy to Jesus. The crowds, gathered around Jesus, were tired and hungry. When Jesus asked Philip about food for the people, Philip realistically related their financial bind: "Eight months' wages would not buy enough bread for each one to have a bite!" (John 6:7).

Overhearing the conversation, Andrew mentioned a boy with a basket lunch of five loaves of bread and two fish. Some people, especially in that specific society, may have dismissed a child as in the way or unimportant. But optimistic Andrew felt that everyone could be useful to Jesus. Andrew's question about the limited supply among so many people (6:9) was not skepticism. He had an optimistic hope, a sense of wonderment that Jesus could multiply the meager amount. Jesus thanked God for the lunch, distributed an ample meal to all the folks, and collected the leftovers. Andrew is an example for us to hand the Lord resources that He will multiply.

Andrew saw individuals in a crowd. Among 5,000–plus people, he noticed one child. Andrew will not let us forget the possibilities in one person.

Pressure of the Wheel: Hospitable Welcome

A few days before Jesus' crucifixion, some Greeks came for the Passover feast in Jerusalem (John 12:20–22). Maybe because of Philip's Greek name, the group approached him for an introduction to Jesus. Philip hesitated. He had heard Jesus talk about other people being in the fold, but he knew Jesus as Israel's Messiah. We cannot fault Philip for his hesitation. The Jews' natural inclination was to dismiss people of other races as useless to God. However, reluctant to dismiss the Greeks, Philip filtered their request through Andrew's common sense and his instinctive ability to know Jesus' message was not limited to the Jews. Andrew knew Jesus never was too busy to turn away a seeker inquiring for the truth. Recognizing that all people needed to find the Messiah, Andrew welcomed the Greeks into Jesus' presence. Probably, the Greeks lingered in the crowd for a while and heard Jesus predict His death (12:23–28). If so, they received a unique serendipity. Since Andrew did not shoo them away, they heard God's voice. Jesus, speaking to His Father said, "'Father, glorify your name!' Then a voice came from heaven, 'I have glorified it, and will glorify it again.' The crowd that was there and heard it said it had thundered; others said an angel had spoken to him" (12:28–29).

 **What We Learn About Transformation from Andrew**

- Not all transformations are emotional or result from crises. Andrew's transformation happened gradually. First, he followed John the Baptist and listened to John's preparatory sermons about the Messiah. Then Andrew listened to Jesus Who reinforced and fulfilled John's message. Finally, without fanfare and with steadiness and strength Andrew decided to serve the Lord. Andrew made decisions based more on his mind and will than on his emotions. The Lord uses all the types of personalities He created.
- Transformed people readily use their gifts without drawing attention to themselves. Lesser known than Peter, whose personality propelled him into the forefront, Andrew's gifts were equally important. Because of his distinct qualities and life experiences, Andrew's transformation was not showy. He wanted people to meet Jesus even if it meant his working in the background. Leaders depend on salt-of-the-earth, dependable vessels like Andrew.

Peter preached and 3,000 people believed. Andrew handed a food basket to Jesus and 5,000 people ate.

Questions to Consider
1. Name one characteristic of Andrew. Tell how God used it to introduce people to Jesus.

2. What evidence in Andrew's life shows his transformation was real although not emotional.
3. What does Andrew's experience indicate about
   our resources?

If you could mold Andrew, what kind of vessel
would you fashion?

CHAPTER 8

Peter

God's plan included a powerful sermon at Pentecost and a shepherd-pastor for the church. He changed an impetuous fisherman with a pendulum personality into a man of staunch convictions and a tender heart.

God's Choice of Clay

Heat, pressure, and upheavals slowly form rocks. When Jesus chose Simon, He knew that the heat, pressure, and upheavals of life's experiences would chisel a rock from a volatile man. Peter's actions and attitudes shifted from cowardice to courage, from strength to instability, from hesitation to hopefulness. Jesus molded Peter into the man He needed for the beginning of the church.

Peter was a family man with a home in Capernaum and a fishing business on the Sea of Galilee. He was strong enough to pull ashore a net full of fish and habitually drowsy enough to sleep through crises. Peter, taught by the Pharisees, was looking for a political Savior. No doubt, the preaching of John the Baptist influenced Peter's receptivity toward Jesus. Still in the recesses of his mind Peter thought the Son of man would have power to destroy the Jews' enemies. Jesus' teachings about a cross seemed incredible. Gradually with Jesus' companionship and discipline, Peter began to appreciate Jesus' mission and message. Peter was inquisitive. His questions gave Jesus the opportunity to teach about:

1. Forgiveness: "Then Peter came to Jesus and asked, 'Lord, how many times shall I forgive my brother when he sins against me? Up to seven times?' Jesus answered, 'I tell you, not seven times, but seventy-seven times'" (Matt. 18:21–22).

2. Rewards: "Peter said to him, 'We have left all we had to follow you!' 'I tell you the truth,' Jesus said to them, 'no one who has left home or wife or brothers or parents or children for the sake of the kingdom of God will fail to receive many times as much in this age and, in the age to come, eternal life'" (Luke 18:28–29).

3. Servanthood: "'No,' said Peter, 'you shall never wash my feet.' Jesus answered, 'Unless I wash you, you have no part with me.' 'Then, Lord,' Simon Peter replied, 'not just my feet but my hands and my head as well!'" (John 13:8–9).

"When he had finished washing their feet, he put on his clothes and returned to his place. 'Do you understand what I have done for you?' he asked them. 'You call me "Teacher" and "Lord" and rightly so, for that is what I am. Now that I, your Lord and Teacher, have washed your feet, you also should wash one another's feet. I have set you an example that you should do as I have done for you. I tell you the truth, no servant is greater than his master, nor is a messenger greater than the one who sent him. Now that you know these things, you will be blessed if you do them'" (13:12–17).

Peter was working when Jesus connected the fisherman's vocation to His mission—fishing for men. Peter may have been attracted to Jesus because an appeal for adventure was a Galilean trait. Although not formally taught or skilled in the law, Peter grasped the compelling significance of the call. He followed Jesus to become a rock-in-the-making.

The Wheel of Circumstances
God saw potential in Peter's clay. He placed Peter on the wheel of circumstances to mold him into a useful vessel.

Pressure of the Wheel: Shaping Stability
With two experiences Jesus immediately began shaping stability in Peter. First, He kindled hope by promising a name change: You are Simon. You will be Cephas (Rock) (John 1:42). Jesus stirred expectation in Peter who probably despaired of ever being stable.

Second, Jesus demonstrated His power over nature as superior to Peter's knowledge of fishing (Luke 5:4–11). Peter had spent the night in a futile attempt to catch fish. When Jesus suggested another try, Peter hesitated. Successful fishing was improbable during the day and in deep water. However, Peter obeyed and pulled in nets heavy with fish. This experience instilled in Peter's mind that Jesus was more than an ordinary man. Being in Jesus' company on a regular basis encouraged steadiness in Peter's personality.

Pressure of the Wheel: Kneading Peter's Flaws
Basically Peter was a good-hearted man and devoted to Jesus. He was not mean-spirited or manipulative. We often identify with the humanness of his weaknesses and his aspirations. With continuous patience, Jesus kneaded Peter's eager exclamations or verbal blunders and impulsive actions. In the margin of my Bible is a comment by an anonymous person: Peter's virtues exaggerated became his faults. Let's personify his qualities and:

- Hear his hospitable enthusiasm irresponsibly suggest to build three tents on the Mount of Transfiguration;
- See his courage jump into a stormy lake to reach Jesus;
- Hear his rebuke to Jesus attempting to deflect Him from the Cross; and
- See his loyalty defend Jesus in Gethsemane.

Jesus molded Peter's sudden inclinations to speak and to act into a pliable vessel.

Pressure of the Wheel: Peter's Highs and Lows

The same difficult teachings of Jesus that caused the crowds to desert Him were to Peter words of truth. Forlornly, Jesus asked the disciples whether or not they would leave Him too. Peter comforted Jesus with a noble declaration, "To whom shall we go? You have the words of eternal life." Peter's reason for his conviction was, "We believe and know that you are the Holy One of God" (John 6:66–69).

Another high moment was Peter's confession of faith, "You are the Christ" (Matt. 16:16). Peter expressed the conviction revealed to him by God. He affirmed Jesus without fear of contradiction. Jesus affirmed Simon by calling him Peter.

The pendulum of emotions swung toward low moments. At the Last Supper, Peter earnestly resolved to stand by Jesus. He had not learned that the flesh was weaker than the spirit. Peter's devotion to Jesus degenerated into a self-confident boast of his permanent allegiance to Jesus. Presuming exemption from temptations, Peter yielded to temporary panic. Three times in the courtyard, he failed to confess his loyalty to Jesus. Simultaneously, Peter denied knowing Jesus, heard the rooster crow, and saw Jesus' look of disappointment. Heartbroken and humiliated for his shameful denials, Peter wept bitterly. No doubt, until his death, Peter remembered the denials every time he heard a cock crow. But balancing the rooster crow was another memory: Jesus prayed for him. "Simon, Simon, Satan has asked to sift you as wheat. But I have prayed for you, Simon, that your faith may not fail. And when you have turned back, strengthen your brothers" (Luke 22:31–32).

Jesus never doubted Peter's repentance or his ability to lead the apostles. Peter's restoration teaches us how the Lord deals with our failure. He uses a simple incident or a commonplace object to arouse a regret or a hope. Then we feel His look of forgiving love. Meditatively sitting beside Peter at the campfire, I thought:

He gave His body,

He shed His blood,

On Calvary.

With joy, I claimed Christ's sacrifice for me.

Time passed.

What happened to the commitment I made on that day?

I fail to pray.

I disobey.

I betray with my actions.

I deny with my words.

I feel like Peter when he heard the cock crow.

Yes! I feel like Peter! There's hope!

In Your eyes, Lord, I see the tender love that will not let me go.

I remember the promises we made—You to save, I to serve.

Savior, through repentant tears, I plead, "Forgive."

Pressure of the Wheel: Peter's Transformation

Around a fire on the shore, Jesus probed Peter's heart with three questions: Do you love Me unconditionally? Truly love Me unconditionally? Love Me like a brother? The questions that reminded

Peter of his failure removed his pride and cowardice. For each question, Peter penitently reaffirmed his love. With renewed trust in Peter, Jesus charged him to express his love in deeds and words—feed and tend the sheep, His followers.

Jesus did not refer to Peter's denials. He did not ask Peter to promise to do better in the future. Jesus pulled from him a confession of love which is the true motive for ministry. Peter's denial did not disqualify him forever from service and from the fellowship of the apostles.

From the conversation between Jesus and Peter, we feel the tense heartwrenching exposure of Peter's soul. We feel the magnanimous compassion of Jesus. Hearing Jesus' second commission, "Follow me," we feel the ecstasy of Peter's finest moment.

Consequently, Peter's next words cause us to gasp. He pointed to John asking, "Lord, what about him?" I sense exasperation in Jesus' reply, "If I want him to remain alive until I return, what is that to you?" (John 21:21–22). Peter! Still consistently inconsistent.

Pressure of the Wheel: Peter, the Rock
On the seashore, Peter had obeyed Jesus' first call, "Follow me." Now three years later, on the same shore, Jesus gave Peter a new start with the same invitation, "Follow me" (John 21:19). Following Jesus, Peter interpreted the phenomena of the Holy Spirit to the hecklers and preached at Pentecost. He performed miracles (Acts 3:1–8) and defied the Sanhedrin (5:27–41). He exposed the deceit of

Simon, the sorcerer (8:20–24) and introduced the Gentiles to the Messiah. He pled for Christian liberty at the Jerusalem council (15:7–10) and strengthened the brethren (Luke 22:32). Until he died a martyr, Peter justified Jesus' promise to make him a rock.

What We Learn About Transformation from Peter

- Jesus keeps in mind His vision for who we are becoming. He encouraged and comforted Peter during the process and He does the same for us.
- Self-confidence and feeling superior to temptation slow our transformation.
- The Lord can mold a person who speaks before thinking into a polished spokesman for the church. Using a concordance, read all the verses pertaining to Peter. Then contrast the man you meet in the Gospels and Acts to the pastor you meet in 1st and 2nd Peter. The exercise is thought-provoking.
- Transformation involves emotional pain and misunderstanding. Peter did not fully understand his change until he had passed through it. The sermon at Pentecost may have been his first knowledge that the Lord could use him.
- The Lord uses transformed people as vessels for transforming the lives of others.

Every day someone placed the crippled man close to the temple gate at three o'clock, the regular prayer meeting time. From necessity, he begged his livelihood from folks on the way to pray. A few people considered him a nuisance. Others thought he demeaned the neighborhood. "A pest," some believed.

One day Peter and John strolled toward the temple. When the beggar asked for money, Peter and John looked directly at him. Their interest encouraged the man to think a hefty donation was possible. When Peter began speaking, "Silver and gold I do not have," the man probably stopped listening. Disappointed and already turning toward someone else, the beggar barely heard Peter continue, "but what I have I give you. In the name of Jesus Christ of Nazareth, walk" (Acts 3:6).

Suddenly Peter grabbed the beggar's right hand. Now imagine being crippled all your life and having a stranger unexpectedly lift you from the ground! That could be very disturbing! One second the man feared; the next, he rejoiced. Instantly his feet and ankles were strong. He jumped, walked, and praised God. The crowd joined him in the wonder and amazement of the moment! (3:7–10).

How did God transform the beggar? Certainly Peter was God's power channel. But the beggar received more than physical healing. Peter voiced hope. If Peter and John had returned home to search under the sofa cushions for a few misplaced coins, the beggar would have received money expecting to remain a beggar. But after Peter's tug on his wrist, he knew he could jump, walk, and praise God through tomorrow and tomorrow.

Peter enabled the man to trust folks again. Daily spurned by others, the beggar probably had lost faith in people. Peter renewed the man's faith in others and in himself.

Peter showed love. Through the years passersby had deposited coins in the beggar's cup to salve a conscience or to gain attention to themselves. To give miserly or generously with a scornful attitude is a possibility. The beggar always felt the contempt. Through Peter, the beggar felt love because God's power is love. God used Peter's handclasp—a human touch—to bring wholeness to a brother. All of us can be vessels of transformation.

Questions to Consider
1. How did Jesus begin to stabilize Peter's personality?
2. Describe a high and a low experience in Peter's life.
3. How is your life similar or dissimilar to Peter's?

If you could mold Peter, what kind of vessel would you fashion?

CHAPTER 9

The Samaritan Woman at the Well

God planned to embrace everyone in love. The Samaritan woman at the well, compared to a sin-smudged earthen jug, was transformed into a clean pitcher of sparkling living water because Jesus cared about one person.

 **God's Choice of Clay**

The women of Sychar, Samaria, gathered each morning at the town well to fill their water pots and to socialize. But the women excluded at least one woman from the neighborly chatter at their morning ritual. The rejected woman came to the well at noon to avoid the sneers of those who gossiped about her carnal lifestyle. Her clay was marred by sin, weariness, and heartaches.

Beneath the woman's disillusionment, Jesus saw a person with a logical, perceptive, and inquiring mind. Beneath her resentment, He saw respect for authority and reverence for her heritage. Beneath her shame, Jesus saw a forthright attitude and a willingness to help those who had abused her. Beneath her depraved value system, He saw a woman of worth. Society considered the woman the most common of clay. Yet of all the women in Sychar, Jesus waited at the well for her. Jesus demonstrated that God is tolerant toward all people. He chose her to receive the remarkable truth about the inner meaning of worship: "God is Spirit, and his worshipers must worship in spirit and in truth" (John 4:24). To her, Jesus proclaimed His identity: "The woman said, 'I know that Messiah' (called Christ) 'is coming. When he comes, he will explain everything to us.' Then Jesus declared, 'I who speak to you am he'" (4:25–26).

The Wheel of Circumstances

God saw potential in the Samaritan woman's clay. He placed her on the wheel of circumstances to mold her into a useful vessel.

Pressure of the Wheel: Divine Appointment

Traveling from Judea to Galilee, Jesus and the disciples chose to follow the unpopular Samaritan Road. At noon, being in the vicinity of Sychar, they decided to eat lunch. While the disciples shopped for food, Jesus waited at the town well. Sychar was built on the ancient city of Shechem where Abraham and Sarah had lived.

Leaning against the well, Jesus might have thought about the historical significance of the place. Elijah, Elisha, and Hosea had labored in and around the area. Jesus had more urgent thoughts. He needed more than food in Sychar. He needed a witness in the town. Someone whose life, when changed dramatically, would make an impression on the people. Jesus anticipated the arrival of the woman who appeared with an earthen jug poised on her shoulder. Perhaps she felt an inner dissatisfaction carefully camouflaged by a hardened demeanor. Jesus used an ordinary conversation with an extraordinary subject matter to knead her life. As the conversation progressed, Jesus' words, beginning with a trickle of refreshing water, bathed her soul.

Pressure of the Wheel: "How can you ask me for a drink?" (John 4:7–9).

The repartee between Jesus and the woman began with a typical "How are you?" Asking for a drink was a familiar request of a fatigued traveler. Tactfully, Jesus put the woman at ease by asking a favor.

Her question revealed a smoldering hate between the Jews and the Samaritans. Her ancestors had been left behind when the Assyrians deported the ten tribes to other parts of their empire. The remaining people "had intermarried with Assyrian invaders and colonists of other nationalities" brought into the area from Assyrian conquests.[11] Orthodox Jews ostracized the hybrid race. To avoid being defiled by the despised Samaritans, biased Jews traveled a long detour between Judea and Galilee.

The woman's question also revealed strict customs of the times. Men and women did not converse in public. Certainly, Jews and Samaritans never would drink from the same jar.

Pressure of the Wheel: "Sir, give me this water" (John 4:10–15).

Jesus disregarded the woman's remark about the dispute between the Jews and Samaritans. Neither was He concerned about the customs. He directed the conversation to the present opportunity when she could ask for life-giving water.

Perplexed, but with respectful curiosity and with practical sense, she inquired about Jesus' ability to obtain the miraculous water without a jug. As she spoke, her logical mind reviewed the history of the well. It was ancient. Jacob had dug the well. His family and their cows had drunk from the well. Great patriarchs had drawn water here. She may have thought, Is this man able to draw deeper? Is he one of them?

Jesus contrasted the temporary physical satisfaction of well water with His permanent thirst-quenching Spirit. The only living water around Sychar flowed from a spring. Although refreshing, thirst returned. She asked from Jesus the same request He had made of her. "Will You quench my thirst?" At the beginning of the conversation, the woman took Jesus' words in a literal sense of water. Now she began to internalize a deeper meaning.

Feel the pathos in her question! "Sir, give me this water." She never again would have to make the lonely walk to the well. Although hardened by life's circumstances, she still was vulnerable to the taunts of the town gossips. What a comfort to have an inner well that would provide security, rest, acceptance, and peace.

Pressure of the Wheel: "I have no husband" (John 4:17).

A strict custom forbade a man and woman to talk in public. If a conversation between strangers seemed necessary, the woman's husband needed to be present. Jesus' request for the woman to call her husband probably seemed irrelevant to her. But it forced her to face and to confess her sin.

Jesus' condemnation of her promiscuity contained a commendation of the woman's truthfulness. Jesus finds something good in all of us. His honest yet kind revelation of her personal life inspired reverence. The woman realized Jesus was no ordinary man—maybe even a prophet. Subdued and ashamed but not angered by Jesus' assessment of her character, she turned the conversation to a theological issue about worship.

Nodding toward Mount Gerizim in the distance, she said, "Our fathers worshiped on this mountain, but you Jews claim that the place where we must worship is in Jerusalem" (John 4:20). Excuses for ignoring personal spiritual needs have not changed, have they? Faced with her own need, the woman talked about her father's religion.

Her comment may have been an attempt to change the subject. Or she may have felt now was the opportunity to discover the truth from a man who might be a prophet. By building a rival temple on Mount Gerizim, the Samaritans had antagonized the Jews. Giving the woman a respite from an intense conversation, Jesus addressed the issue: "You Samaritans worship what you do not know; we worship what we do know, for salvation is from the Jews" (John 4:22).

Jesus assured her that the true way to God is not determined by the location of a particular temple. Repentance and faith is the true way to God. With a mixture of confusion and hope, she expressed a desire to hear the truth from the expected Messiah. In an unexpected moment the Samaritan woman received the truth that is the foundation of all transformation: "'I who speak to you am he'" (John 4:26). Moses had heard Him say His name, "I Am" (Ex. 3:14). The woman at the well was in very favorable company.

When Jesus' disciples returned with food, they felt the electrifying enlightenment of the moment: "Just then his disciples returned and were surprised to find him talking with a woman. But no one asked, 'What do you want?' or 'Why are you talking with her?'" (John 4:27). Still staring in amazement at Jesus, the woman assimilated all that she had heard: Jesus' knowledge of her life, His authority to offer Living Water, and His power to declare the true meaning of worship.

Pressure of the Wheel: "Come, see" (John 4:29).
The woman left her jug at the well but she took the Water of life back to Sychar. Like a well overflowing, the woman's invitation, "Come and see," splashed on everyone she met. Her past was irrelevant. She was a new woman with an urgent message. One woman's witness transformed a town into believers with their own testimony: "They said to the woman, 'We no longer believe just because of what you said; now we have heard for

ourselves, and we know that this man really is the Savior of the world'" (John 4:42).

 **What We Learn About Transformation from the Samaritan Woman**

- Transformation occurs in the presence of Jesus wherever we may meet Him. I met Him as I rode my bike home from Bible school. Pedaling home, I faced my sin, believed Jesus loved me, and asked Him to be my Savior. With a childlike faith, I experienced salvation. The woman at the well knew more of life's burdens, but the steps to her salvation were identical to mine. She faced her sin, trusted the Messiah, and received His life-giving Spirit. Her new life freed her from the social stigma as she shared with the townsfolk, "Come, see."

- Transformation occurs in response to the simple, uncomplicated message of salvation. Jesus' first words to the woman did not remind her of her sinful life. He did not impose Himself on her. He waited until she was ready to hear. With respect and winsomeness, He met her physical and social needs. He revealed her spiritual need only after arousing her curiosity. He was not diverted by theological questions. He recognized that she desired something more than she possessed. He revealed Himself as her hope. The woman left the well with a new heart and good news. She began the process of transformation in the lives of others.

- The woman at the well has a counterpart in your community. Some women still are uncomfortable mingling at specific times or places for fear of meeting certain people. Some women still are engaged in demeaning occupations and activities. Other women yield to radical lifestyles or philosophies. Women battle insecurity and hurt pride from failures in relationships or professions. Many feel the pressure of racial prejudice. Others, ensnared by immorality, live behind a facade of a successful career, civic participation, and church attendance. "Come, see" must be our invitation to these women.

- Transformations occur by crossing barriers. We are not embarrassed that Jesus made friends with a dishonorable woman. We are not surprised that He risked His reputation by crossing race, gender, and social barriers. After all, He was supposed to talk to everybody. That last sentence indicts us. Aren't we supposed to act like Jesus?

We are glad Jesus changed the woman. He gave us a pattern for witnessing. Why, then, do we make long detours around certain sections of the city we consider undesirable? Why do we shun folks we fear will tarnish our reputations?

- Involvement in the transformation of another person through a witness or a ministry fulfills our needs. Jesus forgot His own hunger and thirst as He shared with the woman. Being human we all have certain basic needs that different experiences satisfy. However, seeing someone respond to the Living Water places in priority all other experiences.

Live transformed today! You have a divine appointment at a symbolic well in your community. Hurry there! An unnamed person is approaching you with an empty pitcher.

Questions to Consider
1. Why did Jesus risk His reputation to talk to the woman?
2. Memorize Jesus' witnessing method that led to the woman's transformation.
3. Who is the woman's counterpart in your neighborhood? Pray for an opportunity to share the transforming message of salvation with her.

If you could mold the woman of Samaria, what kind of vessel would you fashion?

Chapter 10

Zacchaeus

God planned to seek and to save the lost. He gave a grasping vessel the gift of giving.

 **God's Choice of Clay**

Zacchaeus's clay had a selfish, covetous, acquisitive quality. He owned a home in Jericho, a city surrounded by palm forests and balsam groves. Jericho was an important center of trade and taxation because the Romans sold the dates and balsam all over the world.

Zacchaeus, a Jew, was the chief tax collector or publican for the Roman government. Publicans paid the government for the privilege of collecting taxes. Gross abuse was commonplace in the system. The rulers assessed a certain amount of money for each district. The tax collector gave Rome the assessment and appropriated the overage. With no laws to keep the revenuers honest, they gouged the public. On the city streets, a collector could make citizens open packages and tax the contents for any amount. Decent citizens would not associate with a person in such an odious occupation. Synonymous with traitors,

and criminals, publicans were excluded from the syna-
gogue. Perhaps Zacchaeus's clay became brittle as he responded with a hard heart to the contempt of the people.[12]

The Wheel of Circumstances
God saw potential in Zacchaeus's clay.
He placed him on the wheel of circumstances to mold him into a useful
vessel.

Pressure of the Wheel:
Jesus Passed Through Jericho
Perhaps Zacchaeus was counting his
profits when he heard the neighbors' ex-
cited chatter about Jesus coming toward
Jericho. Citizens gathered outside the city to await the
arrival of the dignitary. Then they accompanied the honoree back to town in a homemade parade. Looking
through the mansion gates, Zacchaeus saw folks scurry-
ing out the main road to meet the teacher and miracle
worker. With a natural curiosity to see a popular rabbi,
Zacchaeus joined the procession. But taller people
barred his view. Some elbowed their public enemy.
Others ridiculed a man they considered a reject from society. Determined to see Jesus, Zacchaeus ran back to
town and climbed up a sycamore tree along the route.

Pressure of the Wheel: Zacchaeus's Transformation
As the procession passed under the tree, Jesus paused.
He acknowledged Zacchaeus by name and invited
Himself to eat with the outcast. The adulation of Jesus by
the crowd changed to astonishment. In the stunned

silence, we can hear Zacchaeus's sandals scraping against the bark as he scrambled out of the tree. Minutes passed before the crowd caught their breaths enough to murmur, "He has gone to be the guest of a 'sinner'" (Luke 19:7). The self-righteous grumblers, questioning Jesus' choice of a dinner companion, contrasted to Zacchaeus's great joy.

The dinner conversation is unrecorded. They may have talked about eternal life with Luke 19:9–10 being a summary of their discussion: "Jesus said to him, 'Today salvation has come to this house, because this man, too, is a son of Abraham. For the Son of Man came to seek and to save what was lost.'" Zacchaeus's transformation was shown by his actions. He determined to make restitution to all he had robbed and to give a half of his goods to the poor. The name Zacchaeus means pure or innocent. Jesus restored the meanings of pure and innocent that had been stained by sin and corrupted by an immoral occupation. Zacchaeus's transformation is an example of 2 Corinthians 5:17, "If anyone is in Christ, he is a new creation; the old has gone, the new has come!"

What We Learn About Transformation from Zacchaeus

- Transformation requires that a lost person meet Jesus. In the brief encounter between Jesus and Zacchaeus, we learn Jesus' mission and work: "'The Son of Man came to seek and to save the lost'" (Luke 19:10 TEV). Jesus is our example as we help others experience transformation.

- Transformation requires Christians to live with a sense of urgency. Journeying to Jerusalem where He would be crucified, Jesus never would return to Jericho. Zacchaeus was one of the last persons Jesus sought and saved before His crucifixion. Jesus teaches us to be alert in every opportunity to witness and minister. We never know which moment will be our last one to speak a word of regret or confidence; to perform a kind act; to control an abusive attitude; or to break a harmful habit.

In this encounter the fact that Zacchaeus did not delay is important also. Suppose he had waited until the crowd dispersed? Suppose he had waited to ask Matthew, a former tax collector, some questions about Jesus? He might have missed salvation. Divine appointments are realities.

- Transformation is possible for people rejected by society. The opinions of other people should not deter us from association with any person. Jesus' kindness helped ease the barriers. Instead of denouncing Zacchaeus, He showed compassion.
- Transformation does not change a person beyond recognition. Zacchaeus's greed pushed him to increase his wealth. Jesus did not teach that making money was wrong. Money in the hands of Jesus can be a powerful resource for good. The acquisition of money as an end in itself presents a spiritual danger. Zacchaeus chose to transfer his ability to make money to honest goals and to improve society. Zacchaeus challenges us to glorify God with financial success.

Look at another example. Paul had a fighter instinct. He was on a rampage to slaughter Christians. When Christ transformed Paul, He directed Paul's pugnaciousness toward a new purpose. Paul was able to say about his ministry, "I have fought the good fight" (2 Tim. 4:7).

Questions to Consider
1. Name one of society's pressures on Zacchaeus.
2. Why did Jesus dine with Zacchaeus and what was the neighbors' reaction?
3. Which fact in Zacchaeus's transformation do you relate to now?

If you could mold Zacchaeus, what kind of vessel would you fashion?

CHAPTER 11

Jesus' Transformation

For many days I labored to write a lofty theological essay about Christ's transformation as recorded in John 1:14. However, my recurring thought was more simple than sublime. I remembered myself as a 9-year-old cyclist pedaling my bike up and down Ann Street Hill. The hill was always a challenge, especially at noon with the hot July sun sapping my strength.

I remembered riding the bike to Vacation Bible School. During that week of Bible school, I struggled with more than heat and the height of the hill. I contended with the guilt that I was a sinner in need of a Savior. Then one day at noon as the hill loomed into view, the relationship between the baby in the crib and Christ on the Cross connected in my young mind. I asked Jesus to be my Savior.

Through the years I learned more about Jesus. He was Immanuel, God in human form. He became my substitute, my rescuer, my intercessor. He was born to redeem me! Such grace, such undeserved mercy over-flows my heart with praise: Lord, thank You for being more than I can understand. The poetry of Proverbs 8:22–31 (NIV) is a beautiful attempt to personify the more-than-I-can-understand:

The Lord brought me forth as the first of his works,
before his deeds of old;
I was appointed from eternity,
from the beginning, before the world began.
When there were no oceans, I was given birth,
when there were no springs abounding with water;
before the mountains were settled in place,
before the hills, I was given birth,
before he made the earth or its fields
or any of the dust of the world.
I was there when he set the heavens in place,
when he marked out the horizon on the face of the deep,
when he established the clouds above
and fixed securely the fountains of the deep,
when he gave the sea its boundary
so the waters would not overstep his command,
and when he marked out the foundations of the earth.
Then I was the craftsman at his side.
I was filled with delight day after day,
rejoicing always in his presence,
rejoicing in his whole world
and delighting in mankind.

You, Jesus, as the Word, preexisted with God. "In the beginning was the Word, and the Word was with God, and the Word was God. He was with God in the beginning" (John 1:1–2). You were not God-like. You were His image. "He is the image of the invisible God, the first born over all creation" (Col. 1:15). "The Son is the radiance of God's glory and the exact representation of his being, sustaining all things by his powerful word" (Heb. 1:3). You, Lord, possessed God's mind, will, intelligence, power, truth, sufficiency, glory, holiness, blessedness, and majesty.

Lord, thank You for speaking into existence an orderly, harmonious macrocosm. "For by him all things were created: things in heaven and on earth, visible and invisible, whether thrones or powers or rulers or authorities; all things were created by him and for him. He is before all things, and in him all things hold together" (Col. 1:16–17). Infinite space is beyond my comprehension. To visit the most distant galaxies 12,000 billion billion miles from earth, I would have to travel for several billion light years. From that vantage point, I could look in all directions at farther frontiers of space.

One spring, the earth and a meteorite swarm passed in close proximity. On the night of the most publicized shower appearance, a group of young people lay on blankets in our backyard to view the sight. Eventually a meteorite flickered on the horizon. A teenager laughed, "Everybody who saw that one raise your hand." Another said, "Let's wait for the instant replay." For some time, the youth bantered comments back and forth. Gradually, the meteorites increased until they appeared in rapid succession.

They stretched up, zoomed down, hung like brilliant stars. A silent awe settled over the group. The youth responded with a spontaneous antiphonal prayer. One whispered, "Look at all that beauty." Another exclaimed, "And it's just for us to see." One said, "Imagine all the power up there." In response, another said, "That same power lives in me." Still another remarked, "Think about the order that keeps all this in orbit." One answered, "He also directs my life."

In the wee hours of the morning, gazing into the heavens, we all felt at one with the Creator of the universe. We all experientially connected the lights in the sky to "the true light that gives light to every man" (John 1:9).

Meteorites, offering a glimpse of God, never could interpret the complete nature of God. The law, highlighting our sins, that Moses received at Sinai is inadequate to intervene and forgive us. "For since the creation of the world God's invisible qualities—his eternal power and divine nature—have been clearly seen, being understood from what has been made, so that men are without excuse. For although they knew God, they neither glorified him as God nor gave thanks to him, but their thinking became futile and their foolish hearts were darkened" (Rom. 1:20–21).

"In the past God spoke to our forefathers through the prophets at many times and in various ways, but in these last days he has spoken to us by his Son, whom he appointed heir of all things, and through whom he made the universe" (Heb. 1:1–2).

And so the Creator of the meteors, the Author of the law became Immanuel, God with us (Isa. 7:14).

Lord, thank You, for responding to the helplessness of our sinful plight. For our sakes, You did not cling to Your privilege, enrich Yourself, clutch Your treasure, or claim Your deity as God's equal! "Your attitude should be the same as that of Christ Jesus: Who, being in very nature God, did not consider equality with God something to be grasped" (Phil. 2:5–6). You poured out the glory, honor, majesty from Your divine vessel: "And now, Father, glorify me in your presence with the glory I had with you before the world began" (John 17:5). Never reducing Your deity, You chose to reside in common clay. You left Your throne for its footstool, earth, a dust particle in the universe: "This is what the Lord says: 'Heaven is my throne, and the earth is my footstool'" (Isa. 66:1).

Only love caused your selfless concern to redeem unworthy sinners and to receive us into the family of God.

Only love committed You to enter earth immaculately conceived (Luke 1:30–35).

Only love committed You to come to earth to live our lives, suffer our heartaches, face our temptations, and die our death.

Only love combined Your deity with human restrictions and dignified the body as a temple of Your Spirit (1 Cor. 3:16).

Only love compelled Your poverty that we might become rich (2 Cor. 8:9).

Lord, thank You, that as the Word, You gave us access to God's way of life. Adapting to our frailties, You communicated God's grace, truth, mercy, holiness, forgiveness, accessibility, and judgment. When we listen to Your words and look at Your ways, we see God.

Lord, thank You, that Your transformation incarnated a glorious, omnipotent sovereign into an humble, obedient servant: "Who, being in very nature God, did not consider equality with God something to be grasped, but made himself nothing, taking the very nature of a servant, being made in human likeness. And being found in appearance as a man, he humbled himself and became obedient to death—even death on a cross!" (Phil. 2:6–8). Relinquishing Your divine existence to become a servant, You satisfied God's requirement for our salvation.

Your servanthood shames our complacency. Help us to see individuals as You saw Mary and Martha (Luke 10:38–42). Help us show compassion for the crowds as You did in the towns and villages (Matt. 9:35–38). Replace our selfishness with an otherness. Stir us to be available suppliers of God's grace and truth to people snared in lostness or shackled in adversities. Lord, teach us the meaning of Romans 15:1: "We who are strong ought to bear with the failings of the weak and not to please ourselves."

As I studied Scriptures about servanthood, I received a letter from a friend who recently exchanged an administrative position for a more hands-on profession. Her words are thought-provoking: "Being here at Hospitality House is changing my life. A couple of weeks ago, the hose on my washing machine split and water soaked into the carpet in the dining area, the hall, and the bathroom. I was upset.

"But, here at the house, a 19-year-old lay dying from leukemia, and a 39-year-old who was free from cancer on Thursday was rediagnosed on Monday with the disease back full force. When I went home and looked at the carpet mess, it seemed trivial. Here were families dealing daily with life and death and I was really upset over a 'maybe' ruined carpet.

"Well, yesterday, my carpet got fixed and it looks as good as new. In fact, it is cleaner than it has been in a long time. But the 19-year-old died and the 39-year-old is still hospitalized. Being here is helping me get a grip on what really matters in life.

"All things are relative, but all relatives are not things. Each relative who comes here to be a patient in a hospital is dear and precious to someone who comes to stay at our House. Things can usually be fixed; sometimes, people cannot. Hopefully, we are all on our way to learning and remembering this lesson."[13]

Lord, exchanging a heavenly city for the unpretentious, itinerant life of a servant is humility. Your patience and modest behavior shame our arrogance, competitiveness, and wrongful pride in our accomplishments. When selfish impulses surface, remind us that before You carved in Joseph's shop, You called the universe into existence; before You dressed in the robe and sandals of a slave, You wore gleaming garments of a king.

Yielding Your unlimited power, You obeyed God's divine plan. Temporarily accepting the limitations of a human vessel, You identified with our dilemma and qualified to be our sacrifice: "But we see Jesus, who was made a little lower than the angels, now crowned with glory and honor because he suffered death, so that by the grace of God he might taste death for everyone" (Heb. 2:9). Voluntarily You "poured out" Yourself for our sins: "There I will give him a portion among the great, and he will divide the spoils with the strong, because he poured out his life unto death, and was numbered with the transgressors.

For he bore the sin of many, and made intercession for the transgressors" (Isa. 53:12).

"The Word became flesh and made his dwelling among us" (John 1:14) means:
- We have a Redeemer Who by fulfilling the demands of the law, set us free who broke the law: "But when the time had fully come, God sent his Son, born of a woman, born under law, to redeem those under law, that we might receive the full rights of sons" (Gal. 4:4–5).
- We have a new name. Trusting Christ as Savior, we become heirs: "So you are no longer a slave, but a son; and since you are a son, God has made you also an heir" (Gal. 4:7).
- We have a new nature: "Therefore, if anyone is in Christ, he is a new creation; the old has gone, the new has come!" (2 Cor. 5:17). God did not take the good pieces of our lives and rearrange them. He made us new.

Living in a town where cotton is a major crop has helped me understand the concept of a new nature. As I write the season is spring. "Without consulting the calendar, I recognize April. I hear the jerking whir of cotton planters heading toward the fields near [our] home. I smell the freshness of loose earth. I see six-row planters in one operation open the soil, drop [the] seeds, apply fertilizer, and close the furrows. I join the springtime conversation hoping for 180 dry days."

One morning "I tossed [a] teardrop-shaped cotton seed into the path of the planter. Buried! If I never had seen an October harvest, I would have walked away sad on that April morn, questioning the validity of the burial. Why not refine all cotton seed and benefit from the niceties of everything from soap to salad oil? Why? Because the life of more seeds, hidden in the fibers, depends on the death of one.

"Joseph of Arimathea lay the seed of our salvation, Jesus, in a burial place. There away from human touch, God split the seed to produce eternal life! My testimony is that the burial connects with the hope of the harvest.

"[One] morning, the cotton farmer spied the first bloom—the promise of a harvest. One dead seed, exploding by the power of God, split its earth tomb to rise in a new life. A cotton field is a witness to the work of God who brings life out of death, gives it a new form, and produces a harvest.

"One morning, the women attested to a similar yet more momentous experience, 'He is risen' (Matt. 28:6 KJV). Those who trust the resurrection bury sins in His tomb and arise to a new life in Christ (Rom. 6:2–11). We are prepared for a future day when we will see the Lord seated on a white cloud, holding a sickle 'because the time to reap has come, for the harvest of the earth is ripe' (Rev. 14:15)."[14]

- We have a new legal standing and a new family relationship. We are born into God's family through faith in Christ. Our condition is like a baby who needs to grow. At the same time, our position is like an adopted adult who immediately enjoys all spiritual riches in Christ: "But when the time had fully come, God sent his Son, born of a woman, born under the law, to redeem those under law, that we might receive the full rights of sons" (Gal. 4:4–5).
- We have the presence of the Holy Spirit. When we

trust Christ as Savior, His Spirit resides in our human vessel. The Spirit helps us express "Abba Father," a joyful cry of trust and thanksgiving about our relationship with God: "Because you are sons, God sent the Spirit of his Son into our hearts, the Spirit who calls out, 'Abba, Father'" (Gal. 4:6).

- We are rescued from sin and death. Christ's death crushed the power of Satan, the source of sin and death in the world. All of us are a part of a three-act drama: We are born. We live. We die. Death is a grim experience for people who have not found an adequate faith for dying. Christ conquered death through His life, death, and resurrection. He enables us to face death victoriously: "Since the children have flesh and blood, he too shared in their humanity so that by his death he might destroy him who holds the power of death—that is, the devil—and free those who all their lives were held in slavery by their fear of death" (Heb. 2:14–15). Christians look with joy beyond this life to a home in heaven where "He will change our weak mortal bodies and make them like His own glorious body, using that power by which he is able to bring all things under his rule" (Phil. 3:21 TEV).

- We have a High Priest Who intercedes for us. In the Old Testament, the high priest interceded with God on behalf of the people. The priest offered animal sacrifices to appease for the people's sins. However, the priest never completed his work. He repeated the sacrifices time and time again. Christ became both our sacrifice and our High Priest forever. Jesus' once and for all sacrifice never needs repeating: "Such a high priest meets our need—one who is holy, blameless, pure, set apart from sinners, exalted above the heavens. Unlike the other high priests, he does not need to offer sacrifices day after day, first for his own sins, and then for the sins of the people. He sacrificed for their sins once for all when he offered himself. For the law appoints as high priests men who are weak; but the oath, which came after the law, appointed the Son, who has been made perfect forever" (Heb. 7:26–28).

The Old Testament priest identified with sinners because he was a sinner. Becoming a man enabled Jesus to be an understanding High Priest: "For this reason he had to be made like his brothers in every way, in order that he might become a merciful and faithful high priest in service to God, and that he might make atonement for the sins of the people. Because he himself suffered when he was tempted, he is able to help those who are being tempted" (Heb. 2:17–18).

Since Jesus knew the feelings and frustrations of all human experience except sin, He is our advocate and intercessor: "Therefore he is able to save completely those who come to God through him, because he always lives to intercede for them" (Heb. 7:25). When I pray, I imagine the Lord saying to His Father, "Holy Father, hear her prayer. Her prayer is my prayer because she is a part of me."

- We enjoy abundant lives even on days we feel like broken vessels: "I am forgotten by them as though I were dead; I have become like broken pottery" (Psalm 31:12). God's disposition of love, joy, peace, patience, kindness, goodness, faithfulness, gentleness, and self-control (Gal. 5:22–23) resided in Jesus.

In His generosity, God offers the same inexhaustible qualities to all who receive Jesus' explanation of His Father: "No one has ever seen God, but God the One and Only, who is at the Father's side, has made him known" (John 1:18). Life in Christ is rich and ample. As we apply and use Christ's blessings, more blessings continue to flow from His supply. Abundant life began for me at the age of 9. At the foot of Ann Street Hill, an initial transformation saved my soul. When I accepted Jesus as Savior, I found grace, not condemnation or vengeance, but the undeserved, unearned incredible kindness of God.

At the foot of the stairs at the country club, I asked for a better way to live. In retrospect, I'm sure my Intercessor interpreted better as a plea for a closer relationship with Him. In the country club, He transformed my goals and purposes to align with Romans 12:2 (TEV): "Do not conform yourselves to the standards of this world, but let God transform you inwardly by a complete change of your mind."

- Christ offers hope for marred vessels. Remember the potter's field? The yard where potters cast broken crockery? In Jerusalem making pottery was an important business enterprise. The potters hauled bits and pieces of their broken wares to a community refuse dump. The sun faded the clay's color and from a distance the shards resembled dried bones. Hold your thought about the potter's field as you give attention to Judas, the betrayer. I imagine Judas swaggered into the audience with the chief priests and boastfully asked, "'What are you willing to give me if I hand him over to you?' So they counted out for him thirty silver coins" (Matt. 26:15). Judas exchanged an identifying kiss in the garden of Gethsemane for the price of a slave: "If the bull gores a male or female slave, the owner must pay thirty shekels of silver to the master of the slave, and the bull must be stoned" (Ex. 21:32).

At the trial, remorse overwhelmed Judas (Matt. 27:3). Remorse is "annoyance of having miscalculated." Remorse means "convicted by stupidity."[15] Remorseful yet unrepentant, Judas felt self-disgust not godly sorrow.

He tried to return the coins mumbling about innocent blood, but the Sanhedrin's interest in Judas ended once he satisfied their purpose. When they dismissed him with a so-what attitude, Judas flung the coins onto the marble pavement of the temple. "Then he went away and hanged himself" (27:5).

Since the coins represented tainted money, they could not be used for temple business. With the blood money of the Son of God, the chief priests bought the potters' field as a cemetery for strangers who died in Jerusalem. "That is why it has been called the Field of Blood to this day" (27:8).

The Jewish leaders, with the exception of Nicodemus and Joseph of Arimethea, never understood the significance of their purchase. The symbolism is precious to Christians. Because of Jesus' blood, our scarred-with-sin vessels—only worthy of the trash heap—may be reshaped as seems best to the Potter (Jer. 18:4).

• We see God. In Jesus the divine Potter appeared. We are indebted to Philip for an important insight from

Jesus: "Philip said, 'Lord, show us the Father and that will be enough for us.'

"Jesus answered: 'Don't you know me, Philip, even after I have been among you such a long time? Anyone who has seen me has seen the Father. How can you say, "Show us the Father"? Don't you believe that I am in the Father, and that the Father is in me? The words I say to you are not just my own. Rather, it is the Father, living in me, who is doing his work" (John 14:8–10). "The Word became flesh and made his dwelling among us" (1:14) gives us a purpose.

When excavators entered the tomb of a pharaoh, they wondered why marred earthen jars shared conspicuous positions among the gold goblets and gem-studded bowls. When the jars were transferred to a museum, the curator placed them on the back shelves as unimportant historical relics.

One day the curator saw a glint through a crack in the bottom of one the jars. Cracking the base, he discovered some of the crown jewels imbedded in the clay. Excitedly, he broke the bases of the remaining clay jars revealing all the royal gems—jewels in a jar. The only purpose of the jars was to contain the jewels.[16]

A priceless jewel enclosed in a clay container seems inappropriate. Yet this is God's plan. As vessels for the message of salvation, we are expendable. The message matters.

"We who have this spiritual treasure are like common clay pots, in order to show that the supreme power belongs to God, not to us" (2 Cor. 4:7 TEV).

Valuable Vessels

We have this treasure in a container
    made of clay
    commonplace.

God did not choose to put His treasure
In a resplendent pewter vessel
That I could admire
    as it stays neatly on the shelf
    away from involvement.

God did not choose to put His treasure
In a crystal vessel,
I would then be tempted to tap the rim,
    revealing the clear ring
    of exquisite perfection.

God chose to put His treasure
In weak and worthless vessels
Without glory in themselves
    "in order to show that the supreme
    power belongs to God,
    not to us" (2 Cor. 4:7 NIV).

Thank You, Father.

Amen.

Endnotes

1 W. Hershcel Ford, *Simple Sermons on the Christian Life* (Grand Rapids: Zondervan, 1962), 108.

2 Nell L. Kennedy, *Worthy Vessels: Clay in the Hands of the Master Potter* (Grand Rapids: Zondervan, 1988), 41.

3 Ibid., 9.

4 Taken from a speech by Faith Bryan (used by permission of Our Daily Bread, Grand Rapids, MI).

5 Kennedy, *Worthy Vessels*, 133.

6 William Sanford La Sor, *Men Who Knew God* (Glendale: G/L Regal Books, 1959), 2–11.

7 Ibid., 52–53.

8 *Great People of the Bible and How They Lived* (New York: Reader's Digest Association, 1974), 79.

9 Albert Barnes, *Notes on the New Testament: Explanatory and Practical*, (Grand Rapids: Baker Book House, 1951), 283.

10 William Barclay, *The Master's Men* (Nashville: Abingdon, 1991), 44–45.

11 Edith Deen, *All of the Women of the Bible* (New York: Harper & Brothers Publishers, 1955), 196.

12 John Redhead, *Guidance from Men of God* (New York: Abingdon, 1965), 110–11.

13 Letter by Carol Noffsinger (used by permission).

14 Stuart Calvert, "Prayer Patterns," *Royal Service* 88, no. 10 (April 1995): 38, 41.

15 H. D. M. Spence and Joseph S. Excell, eds., *The Pulpit Commentary* (Grand Rapids: Wm. B. Eerdmans Publishing Company), 15:632.

16 C. Roy Angell, *God's Gold Mines* (Nashville: Broadman Press, 1962), 104–5.

CHRISTIAN GROWTH STUDY PLAN

Preparing Christians to Serve

In the **Christian Growth Study Plan (formerly Church Study Course),** this book, *Transformed: Shaped by the Hand of God*, is a resource for course credit in both the Christian Growth category and the Leadership and Skill Development category of diploma plans. To receive credit, read the book, complete the learning activities, show your work to your pastor, a staff member or church leader, then complete the information on the next page. The form may be duplicated. Send the completed page to:

Christian Growth Study Plan
127 Ninth Avenue, North
Nashville, TN 37234-0117
FAX: (615)251-5067

For information about the Christian Growth Study Plan, refer to the current Christian Growth Study Plan Catalog. Your church office may have a copy. If not, request a free copy from the Christian Growth Study Plan office (615/251-2525).

Please check one or both for credit: ☐ CG-0457 (Missions)   ☐ LS-0050 (Woman's Missionary Union)

PARTICIPANT INFORMATION

Social Security Number (USA Only)	Personal CGSP Number*	Date of Birth (Mo., Day, Yr.)
─	─	─ ─

Name (First, MI, Last)

☐ Mr.
☐ Mrs.
☐ Miss

| Address (Street, Route, or P.O. Box) | City, State, or Province | Home Phone ─ ─ | Zip/Postal Code ─ ─ |

CHURCH INFORMATION

Church Name

| Address (Street, Route, or P.O. Box) | City, State, or Province | Zip/Postal Code |

CHANGE REQUEST ONLY

Former Name

| Former Address | City, State, or Province | Zip/Postal Code |

| Former Church | City, State, or Province | Zip/Postal Code |

| Signature of Pastor, Conference Leader, or Other Church Leader | Date |

*New participants are requested but not required to give SS# and date of birth. Existing participants, please give CGSP# when using SS# for the first time. Thereafter, only one ID# is required. *Mail To:* Christian Growth Study Plan, 127 Ninth Ave., North, MSN 117, Nashville, TN 37234-0117. Fax: (615)251-5067